ISRAEL

ABDO
Publishing Company

ISRAEL

by Lisa Owings

Content Consultant
Sanford Silverberg, Professor of Political Science
Catawba College

CREDITS

Published by ABDO Publishing Company, PO Box 398166, Minneapolis, MN 55439.
Copyright © 2013 by Abdo Consulting Group, Inc. International copyrights reserved in all countries. No part of this book may be reproduced in any form without written permission from the publisher. The Essential Library™ is a trademark and logo of ABDO Publishing Company.

Printed in the United States of America,
North Mankato, Minnesota
102012
012013

♻ THIS BOOK CONTAINS AT LEAST 10% RECYCLED MATERIALS.

Editor: Rebecca Rowell
Series Designer: Emily Love

About the Author: Lisa Owings has a degree in English and creative writing from the University of Minnesota. She has written and edited a wide variety of educational books for young people. Lisa lives in Andover, Minnesota, with her husband.

Cataloging-in-Publication Data

Owings, Lisa.
 Israel / Lisa Owings.
   p. cm. -- (Countries of the world)
Includes bibliographical references and index.
ISBN 978-1-61783-630-5
1. Israel--Juvenile literature.   I. Title.
956.94--dc22

2012946075

Cover: The Golden Dome, Jerusalem, Israel

TABLE OF CONTENTS

CHAPTER 1
A VISIT TO ISRAEL

Your body tenses with anticipation as you board the bus that will take you into the heart of Israel: Jerusalem. While your friends prefer tropical isles, rugged wilderness, or sophisticated cities, you have always sought places layered with history and mysticism—places with secrets. Israel holds thousands of years of secrets.

Glimpses of bright limestone flash past your window, and the present seems to be stripped away to reveal the past as you travel deeper into Jerusalem. The bus screeches to a stop. You step outside, squinting in the hot sun, to find the walls of the Old City towering above you. Jerusalem's Old City is home to places sacred to Jews, Muslims, and Christians. You are eager to explore some of them—and much more.

All buildings in Jerusalem must be faced with the area's native limestone.

Vendors and visitors crowd the entrance to Damascus Gate, the main gate into the Old City.

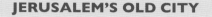

JERUSALEM'S OLD CITY

Jerusalem is Israel's capital city. It is divided into the primarily Arab East Jerusalem and the Jewish West Jerusalem. The Old City is in East Jerusalem. Approximately 5,000 years old, the walled Old City is home to Muslim, Jewish, Christian, and Armenian communities.

THE DOME OF THE ROCK

You walk through the arched gate into the sacred core of Jerusalem and take a moment to get your bearings. You see the Temple Mount, a vast complex where some of the holiest sites in Judaism, Islam, and Christianity are concentrated. The Dome of the Rock sits atop the Temple Mount. A golden oasis in a desert of limestone, its gilded dome stands out in the city's architecture. You head toward the famous Muslim shrine, wanting to beat the afternoon crowds.

You make it through security and climb to the top of the complex. Up close, the splendor of the dome is rivaled only by the intricate inscriptions and brilliantly colored tiles that adorn the walls below. You examine the tiles closely, admiring the grace of the Arabic script and the beauty of the floral patterns painted in rich blues and greens. It is hard to believe this shrine is more than 1,000 years old.

THE WESTERN WALL

Next, you make your way down to Judaism's holiest shrine: the Western Wall, or Wailing Wall. It is all that remains of the ancient temple that once held the tablets inscribed with the Ten Commandments. According to Jewish and Christian beliefs, these tablets were revealed to Moses by God. It forms part of the wall surrounding the Temple Mount.

SACRED STONE

Like many things in Israel, the stone that rests beneath the gleaming Dome of the Rock is sacred to followers of multiple religions. Muslims believe their prophet, Muhammad, ascended into heaven from this rock. Jews regard the stone as the center and foundation of the world. It is also where Abraham, the founder of Judaism, is believed to have prepared to sacrifice his son, Isaac, to prove his trust in God. Today, only Muslims are allowed inside the Dome of the Rock.

You enter the plaza in front of the Western Wall and are immediately struck by the reverence of those in prayer. People of all ages and varied backgrounds have come to this place to feel closer to the divine. As you move toward the expanse of limestone, you see a group of Orthodox Jews. The men, who are separated from the women by a thin barrier called a *mehitza*, wear traditional clothing: black suits and wide-brimmed black hats. They have beards, and their sideburns hang in long curls. You watch them as they study Jewish scripture—the Torah—

The Western Wall attracts visitors day and night.

and pray. You are mesmerized by how the men sway their upper bodies forward and back as they chant.

You squeeze into a narrow space at the wall. The limestone is cool and rough against your palm. A few hardy plants have taken root in the cracks. Tradition seems to have claimed a space between the blocks.

You reach into your pocket and pull out a carefully folded slip of paper on which you have written a prayer. After a couple attempts at respectfully inserting it into a tiny crack along with thousands of other prayers, you give up and unceremoniously jam it in. You look up, expecting disapproving stares, but those around you are standing with their foreheads pressed against the stone, their eyes closed. You do the same and try to let the history of this place seep through your skull.

Suddenly, enchanting music fills the air. It seems to come from all directions. You recognize the language as Arabic. It is the Muslim call to prayer. You listen quietly for a few moments. You step back from the wall to watch the steady movement of Muslim families toward the al-Aqsa Mosque, which also occupies the Temple Mount.

> A recording or a Muslim crier known as a muezzin calls Muslims to prayer five times a day.

CLOSE QUARTERS

Your stomach growls as you leave the complex. It is time to find some food. As you wander through the narrow streets of the Muslim Quarter, you cannot escape the heavy scent of Middle Eastern spices. Market stalls are everywhere. Locals and tourists alike haggle with the vendors. You stop at a stall where a man is selling an Israeli favorite: falafel, or balls of fried chickpeas. You watch as he scoops it into a pita—a type of flat bread that opens like a pocket and is a staple of Middle Eastern cuisine— and nod in agreement as he loads on chopped cucumbers and tomatoes, sauces, and other condiments.

Munching happily, you continue through the souks, or open markets, of the Muslim Quarter. The celebratory atmosphere here sharply contrasts the solemnity of the Temple Mount. Arabic music and shopkeepers' calls echo through the streets. You pass shop after shop overflowing with goods of all kinds. Women run their hands over brightly colored fabric. Children gaze longingly at mountains of sweets. Men bargain over piles of fresh produce and aromatic herbs. People jostle you as they brush past, but you are too excited to mind.

THE CHURCH OF THE HOLY SEPULCHRE

Next, you meander through the quieter Jewish Quarter and the Armenian Quarter, where people from in and around the Asian country of Armenia have settled, on your way to the Christian Quarter, where you have one last stop to make. The dual domes of the Church of the Holy Sepulchre rise above a small courtyard. Christians built this church over the place where they believe the founder of their religion—Jesus Christ—was crucified, buried, and later rose from the dead. You move slowly through the

APPROPRIATE DRESS

At Israel's holy sites and within conservative religious communities, tourists are expected to dress respectfully. Both men and women must have their shoulders covered and wear long pants or skirts. Tourists are sometimes harassed for wearing inappropriate clothing, and they can also be denied entrance to holy sites.

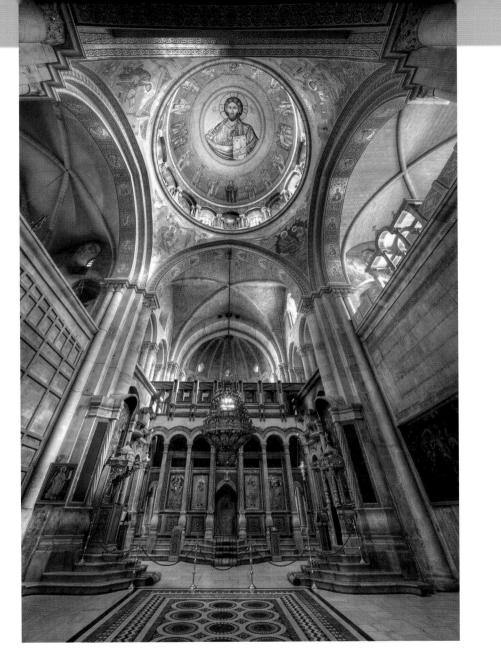

Interior of the Church of the Holy Sepulchre

candlelit building, pausing before shrines where pilgrims kneel in prayer and stopping often to admire the ornate religious artwork. Soon, you are in the cavernous room beneath the main dome. Hushed voices echo. You join the queue of people waiting to enter the chamber where Christ's tomb lies. As you pass through the dimly lit shrine, you are again swept up in the mystical aura that seems to surround everything in the Old City.

You emerge as the sun is just beginning to set. You wind through the tangled streets toward the city walls. When you glance back one last time at the golden Dome of the Rock, it seems to glow from within. During the ride back to your hotel, you reflect on the events of the day. It was inspiring to see so many people of different cultures and backgrounds sharing this incredible city.

ISRAEL AND JUDAISM

Israel occupies sacred ground. Its land is precious to people of many faiths, and they have fought over it for millennia. Today, Israel is especially dear to Jews. It was established as a Jewish state and is the only country in the world where Judaism is the primary religion. Jews believe that, in ancient times, God promised the land of Israel to them. After generations of conflict, hardship, and discrimination, they officially claimed it as their homeland in 1948.

More than three-fourths of Israelis are Jewish, meaning they belong to the same ethnic group and hold the same religious beliefs as the ancient people of Israel.[1] The influence of the culture and belief system

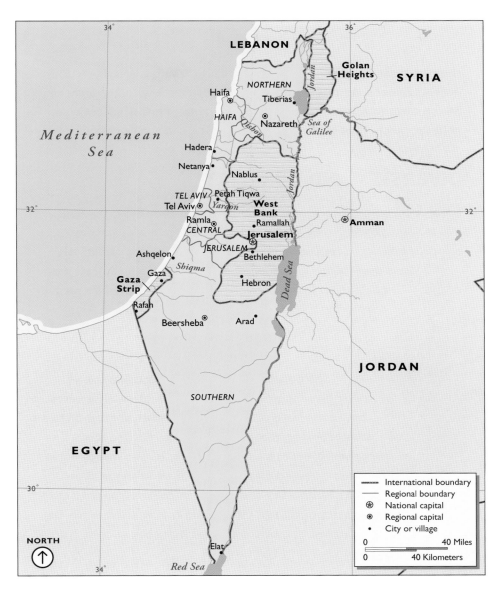

Political Boundaries of Israel

they share can be seen in all aspects of daily life: the language, the food, the holidays, the clothing, and the political battles. Jews come from all over the world to experience the special sense of belonging they feel in Israel.

DIVERSITY AND CONFLICT

Israel occupies a region formerly known as Palestine. Since the 600s, this region has been home to Arabs, an ethnic group whose members primarily follow the religion of Islam. Arabs have been in conflict with Jews over this holy land for centuries—long before Israel was established. Today, Israel has acquired control of the vast majority of what once was Palestine. Jews and Arabs continue to fight over the right to claim the holy land as their own.

Temple Mount is known as Al-Harm al-Sharif in Arabic and Har Ha-Bayit in Hebrew.

You notice the effects of this conflict: the ever-present armed Israeli soldiers, the walls erected between Jewish and Arab communities, and the heated debates among impassioned citizens. For the most part, though, Israel is a friendly place. Its people are warm and open. Its cities—crowded with natives, immigrants, and tourists—are proof that diversity and peace can coexist. You have never visited a country so rich in culture, history, and tradition. After one day, you have barely scratched the surface of what Israel has to offer. You cannot wait to continue your adventure.

SNAPSHOT

Official name: State of Israel

Capital city: Jerusalem

Form of government: parliamentary democracy

Titles of leaders: president (head of state); prime minister
(head of government)

Currency: new Israeli shekel

Population (July 2012 est.): 7,590,758
World rank: 97

Size: 8,019 square miles (20,770 sq km)
World rank: 154

Languages: Hebrew (official), Arabic (official for Arab minority),
English (most common foreign language)

Official religion: none, though Judaism is considered the religion of Israel

Per capita GDP (2011, US dollars): $31,400
World Rank: 41

CHAPTER 2

GEOGRAPHY: A VARIED LANDSCAPE

Israel is a relatively small country. Its 8,019 square miles (20,770 sq km) make it slightly bigger than the US state of New Jersey.[1] Israel has an astounding array of geographic features and microclimates. Traveling through the country from north to south, visitors will discover rugged mountains, fertile plains, and vast expanses of desert. Golden beaches in the east rise into green hills before the land dips into the river valley to the west. In winter, Israelis can easily escape the frigid highlands with an hour's drive to the sun-drenched shores of the Dead Sea.

Israel's varied landscape is defined by what it lacks: water. The Jordan River, which fills the Sea of Galilee, is the main source of freshwater in Israel. Israelis rely heavily on the river for agricultural and household use, pumping large quantities of its water into the drier regions of the country. Overuse of this precious resource—in addition to

The lush green and snowcapped mountains in this valley are a good example of the contrasts in Israel's geography.

frequent periods of drought—makes water shortages a continual threat. Despite these concerns, Israelis have managed to turn their country into a land of abundance.

ISRAEL ON THE MAP

Israel is a narrow sliver of the Middle East along the Mediterranean Sea. Its location at the junction of Europe, Africa, and Asia—as well as at the cultural center of the monotheistic world—makes Israel far more important than its diminutive size suggests.

Israel is divided into six districts: Central, Haifa, Jerusalem, Northern, Southern, and Tel Aviv.

Israel shares its borders with four countries: Lebanon to the north, Syria to the northeast, Jordan to the east, and Egypt to the southwest. The Mediterranean Sea is located on Israel's western coast. Southern Israel tapers to a point that dips into the Gulf of Aqaba, an inlet of the Red Sea. This point drives a wedge between Egypt and Jordan.

Israel also shares borders with two largely autonomous Palestinian territories: the West Bank and the Gaza Strip. The West Bank was once administered by Jordan, and the Gaza Strip was once administered by Egypt. After acquiring these territories in 1967 as a result of an armed conflict, Israel agreed to gradually relinquish them to the Palestinian Authority in exchange for peace. As of 2012, the permanent status of these territories had yet to be determined.

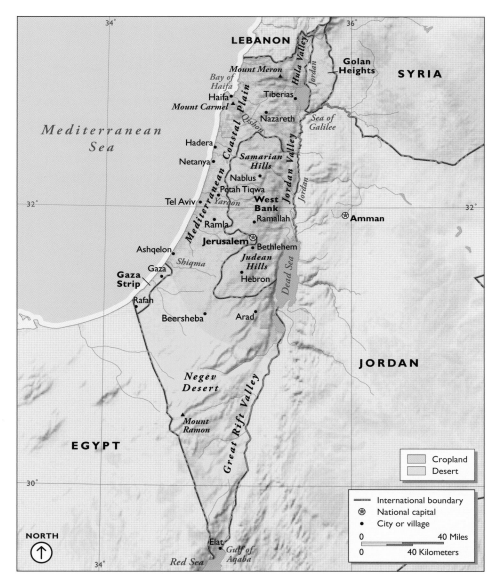

LEBANON

Mount Meron ▲

Bay of Haifa

Haifa •

Mount Carmel ▲

Hadera •

Netanya •

Samarian Hills

Nablus •

Petah Tiqwa •

Tel Aviv •

Ramla •

Ashqelon •

Shiqma

Gaza •

Gaza Strip

Rafah •

Beersheba •

Negev Desert

Mount Ramon ▲

EGYPT

Mediterranean Sea

Mediterranean Coastal Plain

Qishon

Nazareth •

Tiberias •

Hula Valley

Golan Heights

SYRIA

Sea of Galilee

Jordan Valley

Jordan

West Bank

Ramallah •

Jerusalem ⊛ • Bethlehem

Judean Hills

Hebron •

Arad •

Dead Sea

⊛ **Amman**

JORDAN

Yarqon

Great Rift Valley

Elat •

Gulf of Aqaba

Red Sea

NORTH
↑

34°

36°

32°

32°

30°

34°

| | Cropland |
| | Desert |

— — — International boundary
⊛ National capital
• City or village

0   40 Miles

0   40 Kilometers

Geography of Israel

THE LAY OF THE LAND

Israel encompasses four major geographic regions: Mediterranean coastal plain, highlands, Negev, and Great Rift Valley. The coastal plain sweeps along the Mediterranean Sea. Many of Israel's cities—including Tel Aviv and Haifa—stand on this flat, narrow strip of land. Sandy beaches at the water's edge give way to fertile farmland dotted with vineyards and citrus groves farther inland.

Mountains and hills cover northern and central Israel. The mountains of Galilee in the far north contain Israel's highest point, Mount Meron. Its peak rises 3,963 feet (1,208 m) above sea level and is occasionally dusted with snow.[2] Across the plains to the south of Galilee rises the Mount Carmel range, which extends from Haifa to the upper reaches of the West Bank. The Yarqon and Qishon Rivers flow west through mountain valleys and empty into the Mediterranean Sea. A ridge of hills runs north to south through the center of the country, stretching from the West Bank to the northern edge of the Negev Desert. Jerusalem is nestled among these hills, which are referred to as the Samarian Hills north of Jerusalem and the Judean Hills to the south.

The Negev Desert occupies the southern half of Israel. Its sandy expanse grows increasingly arid toward the southern tip of the country. Few people live in the desert. Over millions of years, wind and water have sculpted the land into craters, cliffs, and subtly striped hills. The Red Sea quenches the southernmost sands of the Negev. The sunny city of Elat basks on the coast.

The Negev Desert at Qumran, Israel

A crack in the earth's crust forms a deep valley along the eastern border of Israel. The Great Rift Valley slices from the headwaters of the Jordan River through Mozambique in eastern Africa. The Jordan River flows south through northern Israel into the Sea of Galilee, forming part of Israel's eastern border. It exits this large freshwater lake and continues

along the border with Jordan until it empties into the Dead Sea.

The Dead Sea is one of the most interesting geographic features in Israel. This body of water is so salty nothing but bacteria can live in it. Its high salt content makes floating easy, and its mud and minerals are believed to have healing powers. These unique qualities draw masses of tourists to the Dead Sea each year.

THE DEAD SEA

The Dead Sea is almost nine times saltier than seawater. Because the lake has no outlet, water is trapped there until the sun causes it to evaporate. During evaporation, the salt and minerals dissolved in the water are left behind. These minerals form crystals along the shore and bottom so plentiful that factories and spas have sprung up around the lake, mining the minerals to produce chemicals, fertilizers, and beauty products. The Dead Sea is in danger of drying up. As more and more water from the Jordan River is diverted for irrigation, less and less water makes it into the Dead Sea.

MAJOR CITIES

Approximately two-thirds of Israelis live in three major cities: Tel Aviv, Haifa, and Jerusalem.[3] Each city has a distinctly different character. The Israelis have a saying: "In Jerusalem we pray, in Tel Aviv we play, and in Haifa we work."[4]

The Jordan River

Tel Aviv's beaches attract thousands of people.

Tel Aviv is Israel's largest and most sophisticated city, and it
has become an important economic and cultural center. Its modern
skyscrapers overlook the Mediterranean Sea. This beachside city has

also become the primary destination for Israelis and tourists seeking entertainment and a vibrant nightlife.

Haifa is the second-most populous city in Israel. Located in northern Israel, Haifa is the country's primary port on the Mediterranean. Israelis commute there to work in factories that turn out food products, steel parts, cement, textiles, and other goods. Haifa also boasts diverse residential communities and institutions of higher learning.

Jerusalem is Israel's most famous city and its spiritual center. Its holy sites attract residents with varying ethnicities, religious beliefs, and languages. Ancient tradition reigns within the walls of the Old City, while high-rise buildings, traffic jams, and other markers of modernity dominate the rest of Jerusalem.

While Jerusalem's many religious sites bring myriad people together, an attitude of divisiveness prevails. The city is currently split between Jews and Arabs, who continue to battle for total control.

SEASONS AND CLIMATE

Israel experiences mild, rainy winters between October and April and hot, dry summers between May and September. Due to the country's geographic diversity, the climate varies from region to region. The Mediterranean coast is pleasantly warm and humid year-round. Northern Israel is cooler in summer and receives more rain—and sometimes snow—in winter.

The Negev Desert, Jordan Valley, and Red Sea coast are inhospitably hot and dry, with summer temperatures soaring above 100 degrees Fahrenheit (38°C) and virtually no rain.[5] In addition to droughts and searing heat, these areas are prone to other weather extremes. Sandstorms frequently sweep across the desert, and dangerous flash floods are common in winter.

AVERAGE TEMPERATURE AND PRECIPITATION

Region (City)	Average January Temperature Minimum/Maximum	Average July Temperature Minimum/Maximum	Average Precipitation January/July
Northern Israel/ Mediterranean Coast (Haifa)	52/61°F (11/16°C)	76/84°F (24/29°C)	5.1/0.0 inches (13/0.0 cm)[6]
Central Israel (Jerusalem)	40/51°F (4/11°C)	64/81°F (18/27°C)	5.5/0.0 inches (14/0.0 cm)[7]
Negev Desert (Beersheba)	46/60°F (8/16°C)	71/90°F (22/32°C)	1.4/0.0 inches (3.6/0.0 cm)[8]
Southern Negev/ Red Sea Coast (Elat)	50/68°F (10/20°C)	80/102°F (27/39°C)	0.1/0.0 inches (0.3/0.0 cm)[9]

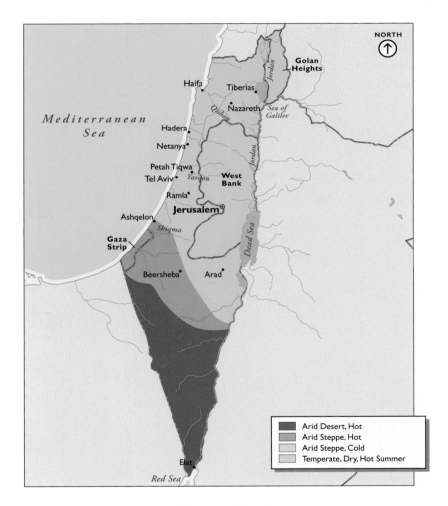

Climate of Israel

CHAPTER 3

ANIMALS AND NATURE: PARADISE REGAINED

The mountain gazelle is one of Israel's signature animals. Although it is classified as a vulnerable species and is rare or extinct in many surrounding countries, the mountain gazelle has found shelter in Israel. It is a protected species in the country, and despite habitat loss and other threats, Israeli mountain gazelles number approximately 3,000.[1]

Small herds of mountain gazelles travel across northern and central Israel. They graze on hardy plants, especially acacia trees. Their ability to survive for long periods without water allows them to flourish in Israel's dry Negev and Jordan Valley regions. Mountain gazelles are slender, with long necks and ridged horns that young males use to fight over mates. If a mountain gazelle encounters a hungry wolf or jackal, it can sprint up to 50 miles per hour (80 km/h) to escape.[2]

Mountain gazelles live in Israel's desert areas.

Predation is just one of the major threats facing Israeli mountain gazelles. After thousands of the gazelles succumbed to foot-and-mouth disease in 1985, their population has continued to decline. Construction and other human activities have resulted in habitat loss. The reduced flow of the Jordan River makes it increasingly difficult for the plants gazelles eat to grow. Hunting—legal and illegal—has also taken a toll on Israel's mountain gazelle population. Legal protection and multiple nature reserves may help this symbol of Israel grow in number.

HIGHLANDS AND PLAINS

Israel is home to far more than the mountain gazelle. The country's wildlife reflects the diversity of its landscape. More than 2,800 species of plants have taken root in Israel's varied soils.[3] The country is also home to approximately 100 species of mammals, 100 species of reptiles and amphibians, and 500 species of birds.[4] Even the farthest reaches of its desert teem with life.

The highlands and plains are lush and green. Oak trees and evergreen shrubs soften the mountains and hills of northern Israel. Sycamore figs have grown in the region since biblical times. During the rainy season, the highlands are graced with bright blooms. Irises, daisies, hyacinths, crocuses, lupines, and poppies decorate the hillsides. The plains are largely cultivated, and fruit trees blossom there in early spring, their flowers replaced by oranges and olives.

Olive trees thrive in areas of Israel.

Other species of gazelle join the mountain gazelles in the highlands. Wild boars, badgers, and foxes keep to wooded areas. Named for their distinctive coats, weasel-like marbled polecats slink through the hills in search of food. Wetlands in the Hula Valley, the northernmost part of the

HULA VALLEY

Israel's wetlands are situated in the Hula Valley, which makes up the part of the Jordan Valley north of the Sea of Galilee. These wetlands once covered approximately 12 square miles (31 sq km) and surrounded a freshwater lake.[5] The area was home to water buffalo, wild boars, and migratory birds of all kinds. Water lilies bloomed throughout the valley. In the 1950s, Israelis began draining water from the Hula Valley, reclaiming the land and water for agricultural use. They left part of the area untouched as a nature reserve. Although the region's farmland was greatly improved, many Israelis would like to see the Hula Valley returned to its natural state.

Great Rift Valley, are a haven for aquatic birds, including cranes, egrets, and pelicans.

DESERT

Vegetation in the Negev Desert and the southern part of the Jordan Valley is scarce. However, acacia trees, cacti, succulents, and other drought-tolerant plants survive. Farmers often use the few oases in the Negev to grow date palms.

Wild goats called ibex ramble over the northern Negev. The Nubian ibex has long, curved horns. Desert gazelles also live in the Negev and in the arid rift valley. Caracals and the occasional leopard are fierce desert predators, and hyenas scavenge their kills. The fennec is the smallest type of fox. Its large ears help keep it cool during the day, while its thick fur keeps it warm at night. Rodent-like hyraxes sunbathe on rocks. They must watch out for

A hyrax soaks up the sun at Ein Gedi Nature Reserve.

MEDITERRANEAN INVADED

The Mediterranean Sea is currently under siege by invasive species. According to scientists at Israel's National Institute of Oceanography, a combination of factors is to blame. The Suez Canal, which opened in 1869 and links the Mediterranean Sea with the Red Sea, provides a corridor through which Red Sea marine life can easily pass into the Mediterranean. Additionally, global climate change has caused the Mediterranean Sea to warm, making it more hospitable to these foreign invaders and less hospitable to native life. Scientists are concerned that invasive species will eventually outcompete native species. This problem, in addition to overfishing and coastal development, could cause many Mediterranean species to become extinct.

the deadly saw-scaled viper and other venomous snakes. Tortoises and lizards can also be spotted on the sands of the Negev. Lizards called agamas turn brilliant shades of blue, red, and yellow when they are ready to mate.

SEAS AND LAKES

Israel's seas and freshwater lakes are homes to myriad aquatic life. Colorful damselfish swim in the Sea of Galilee along with barbells, bottom-feeding blennies, catfish, and a type of tilapia often called St. Peter's fish or comb fish. Mouthbreeders can also be found. Mouthbreeders have a unique way of raising young: the mother lets her eggs mature inside her mouth.

A hawksbill turtle swims along a coral reef in the Red Sea.

Groupers begin their lives as females and later become males.

Off the Mediterranean coast, anchovies, bluefin tuna, groupers, hake, and sea bass struggle for survival, endangered by multiple factors. Sea turtles occasionally surface to breathe. Rays glide majestically through the warm waters while sharks dart after prey. Divers can spot octopuses, jellyfish, eels, and lizard fish. Shellfish such as crabs and shrimp are also common in the Mediterranean Sea.

Corals have built an underwater paradise along Israel's Red Sea coast. The reefs provide shelter for jewel-toned fish, delicate anemones, and sea turtles, including the critically endangered hawksbill turtle. Manta rays glide through the water, and huge humphead wrasses drift in search of small shellfish to eat. Giant whale sharks sometimes make their way into the Red Sea. They open their massive jaws to let in plankton, while their smaller relatives feast on the plentiful reef fish. The port city Elat has a site where visitors can watch and meet dolphins.

SKIES

Its location at the center of three continents makes Israel an important stop for migrating birds. In the fall and spring, the skies above the Mediterranean coast and the Jordan Valley fill with flocks of winged travelers. More than 500 million birds fly over Israel on their way to spend winters in Africa and summers in Europe or Asia.[6] The hundreds of different species include cranes, pelicans, storks, gulls, flamingos, and terns. Eagles, falcons, sparrows, larks, buntings, and warblers also pass through Israel on their journeys.

Bird-watchers come from all over the world to witness Israel's bird superhighway. They gather near Elat or around the wetlands in the Galilee region. While most Israelis appreciate their feathered visitors, the impressive numbers of birds can also cause problems. Pilots of commercial and military aircraft must be extra careful to avoid collisions.

THE HOOPOE

The hoopoe is Israel's national bird. Its body is a rosy brown, and black and white stripes cover most of its wings and its tail. Its orange crest is tipped in black. The hoopoe is approximately 11 inches (28 cm) long, and its call sounds similar to its name.[7] It spends most of its time on the ground searching for insects and worms to eat.

Hoopoes are known for flattening themselves along the ground with their wings splayed behind them and their beaks pointed straight up. Some experts believe the birds assume this posture when they feel threatened. Others claim the hoopoes are simply sunbathing.

ENVIRONMENTAL THREATS AND CONSERVATION EFFORTS

Although plants and animals abound in the country's highlands, deserts, seas, and skies, much of Israel's biodiversity has been lost. Long ago,

hippopotamuses waded in the Jordan River, wild horses galloped across the Negev, and cedar forests shaded northern Palestine. Human settlements caused the gradual disappearance of these species and many others. Today, concerned Israelis are working to reintroduce some of the flora and fauna that once thrived in their land.

Israel is in the process of battling several threats to its environment. As the country's human population increases, its wildlife populations dwindle. To combat the loss of biodiversity, the Israel Nature and Parks Authority has designated approximately one-fifth of the country's land area as protected, including nature reserves and national parks.[8] The Hai Bar reserve

NATIONAL PARKS

Israel has 44 national parks.[9] The most well-known include Masada National Park and En Gedi Nature Reserve and National Park. Both are located next to the Dead Sea. Masada National Park preserves a palatial fortress built by King Herod more than 2,000 years ago. The fortress was also the place where the last Jewish rebels, resigned to a losing battle against Roman invaders, allegedly committed suicide rather than submit to Roman rule. En Gedi boasts freshwater springs, streams, and waterfalls. The park protects the habitat of acacia trees and other local plants and provides a home for ibex, wolves, leopards, and other mammals.

The hoopoe's markings are unmistakable.

north of Elat is dedicated to breeding endangered species, including Asiatic and African wild asses, Arabian and scimitar-horned oryx, and addaxes. Its counterpart on Mount Carmel concentrates on rebuilding populations of Armenian wild sheep, Persian fallow deer, roe deer, and numerous birds of prey. Some of these animals are eventually released into the wild.

Efforts have also been made to replenish Israel's forests. More than 240 million trees—including carob, almond, cypress, cedar, eucalyptus, and pine—have been planted since the early twentieth century.[10]

The addax goes without drinking water most of its life.

Pollution is another major environmental concern in Israel. Air pollution has contributed to increased rates of respiratory illness, cancer, and other diseases. And water pollution compounds the threat to Israel's already limited water supply. Israel has passed legislation to regulate harmful emissions and is improving sewage treatment facilities.

Some of Israel's most promising conservation efforts have been in developing alternative sources of water. Treated wastewater, while not suitable for drinking, can be used for irrigation. Approximately 75 percent of Israel's sewage water is recycled for agricultural use.[11] Israelis are also learning to make the most of their saltwater resources. Several desalination facilities have opened along the Mediterranean coast to

A mother ostrich watches over her young as they graze at the Hai Bar reserve.

ENDANGERED SPECIES IN ISRAEL

According to the International Union for Conservation of Nature, Israel is home to the following numbers of species that are categorized by the organization as Critically Endangered, Endangered, or Vulnerable:

Mammals	15
Birds	13
Reptiles	9
Amphibians	1
Fishes	36
Mollusks	7
Other Invertebrates	53
Plants	0
Total	134[12]

remove the salt from seawater, producing freshwater pure enough for drinking. Capturing flood runoff and rainwater and tapping groundwater resources are other promising solutions for increasing the availability of freshwater in Israel.

Israel opened a desalination plant in Hadera with the goal of relieving the nation's ongoing water shortage.

CHAPTER 4

HISTORY: THE BATTLE FOR THE HOLY LAND

Israel's history is long and complex. It is fraught with war, religious zeal, and the yearning for peace and a place to call home. The epic battle for the Holy Land has raged for millennia between many of the world's great empires and religions. The battle continues in modern Israel, with Jews and Arabs struggling to live together after centuries of conflict. For now, lasting peace remains a hope for the future.

CRADLE OF CIVILIZATION

Modern-day Israel is part of the Fertile Crescent, an area of the Middle East where many of the earliest human civilizations flourished. Humans have inhabited the area since the early Stone Age. Human remains

Artifacts from ancient people discovered in the Jordan River valley

PREHISTORIC TEETH

In December 2010, archaeologists from Tel Aviv University discovered what might be the oldest human remains ever found. The teeth they took from a cave near Israel's Ben-Gurion International Airport are approximately 400,000 years old. The archaeologists are still scouring the cave for further evidence that its occupants were truly Homo sapiens. Such evidence would suggest that the Middle East—not Africa—was home to the earliest modern humans.

found in caves in Israel's Mount Carmel range in the 1930s are more than 90,000 years old.

Over time, these early hunter-gatherer cave dwellers learned to grow crops and domesticate animals to supplement their food supply. By 8000 BCE, they were building small towns, including Jericho, which now lies in the West Bank. Israel's story begins in approximately 2000 BCE, when, according to the Hebrew and Christian Bibles, the Jewish patriarch Abraham moved from his homeland of Ur (present-day Iraq) and settled in Canaan, the area that became known as Palestine.

THE PROMISED LAND

Abraham was the wealthy leader of a seminomadic Hebrew-speaking group that traveled with herds of camels, sheep, and goats. According to the book of Genesis, the first book in the Bible, God summoned

An artist's depiction of God telling Abraham to go to Canaan

THE BIBLE AS A HISTORY BOOK

The Bible is an important historical text. Its pages tell the stories of people, places, and events of ancient times. However, because the Bible is made up of a collection of manuscripts written by different people at different times, and because this collection of manuscripts has been altered, edited, and translated over time, it is difficult to know how accurately the Bible portrays history. Archaeological discoveries in and around Palestine have helped historians and believers alike better understand this sacred book. For example, a drought in the 1980s exposed an ancient-looking boat in the Sea of Galilee. Archaeologists dated the boat to between 100 BCE and 70 CE. The boat matches the biblical description of those in which Jesus and his disciples crossed the Sea of Galilee. The Galilee Boat, or Jesus Boat, is now on permanent display so tourists can enjoy what may truly be a glimpse into the biblical past.

Abraham to a land where he would become the founder of a new nation. Abraham obeyed the summons, traveling from Mesopotamia to a place called Canaan, which corresponds approximately to modern-day Israel and the West Bank. God promised this land to Abraham's descendants.

Abraham had a son named Isaac whose son—Abraham's grandson—was named Jacob. God later renamed Jacob Israel. His sons founded the 12 tribes of Israel, whose members called themselves Israelites. Between 1600 and 1400 BCE, drought and famine drove the Israelites out of Canaan and into Egypt, where many were forced into slavery. In approximately 1250 BCE, the Israelites escaped from their Egyptian oppressors, following their divinely appointed leader, Moses, on the long journey back to the land of Israel.

Over the following centuries, the Israelites gradually defeated the Canaanites and took over their land. In approximately 1020 BCE, the tribes of Israel formed a united army under King Saul when faced with the threat of the Philistines, a more powerful enemy. The first Israelite king and his army were defeated, but Saul's successor, King David, conquered the Philistines and maintained unity among the tribes of Israel. Under David, the Kingdom of Israel stretched from the tip of the Red Sea to the banks of the Euphrates River in modern-day Syria. David's son, Solomon, succeeded him in approximately 965 BCE. Solomon is best known for building the first Jewish temple in Jerusalem, known today as the Temple of Solomon or simply the First Temple.

DIVIDED AND CONQUERED

After Solomon died in approximately 930 BCE, his kingdom split into the Kingdom of Israel in the north and the Kingdom of Judah in the south. The Kingdom of Israel prospered until the Assyrians came to conquer the land. By approximately 732 BCE, the Assyrian Empire had claimed the Kingdom of Israel and exiled its people. A similar fate befell the Kingdom of Judah in 586 BCE, when King Nebuchadnezzar II led the Babylonians in an attack on Jerusalem. The Babylonians destroyed the temple Solomon had built and forced the remaining Israelites into exile. This was the beginning of the Diaspora, which is the scattering of Jews outside Palestine. It was also the beginning of the Jews' collective yearning to return to their homeland.

In 538 BCE, the Persians defeated the Babylonians, and King Cyrus the Great of Persia welcomed the return of the Jews. Many did come back to Judah, and between 520 and 515 BCE, they built the Second Temple where the first had fallen to the Babylonians. This Jewish community enjoyed relative autonomy, or independence, until 63 BCE, even as their homeland changed hands. Alexander the Great conquered Judah in 332 BCE, and the Jews later fell under the rule of the Egyptians in 301 BCE and the Syrians in 175 BCE. The Syrians lost control of Judah in 129 BCE, and the Jews gained sovereignty over their homeland for several decades.

In 63 BCE, the Romans seized Jerusalem, and Judah was eventually swallowed up by the Roman Empire. The Romans appointed Herod king of Judah, which they called Judea. During his reign from 37 to 4 BCE, the Jews were content, but they tired of Roman rule within decades of Herod's death. A group of Jews launched a rebellion in 66 CE that the Romans brutally crushed. The rebellion took place approximately 30 years after the death of Jesus Christ, and Christianity was taking hold in the region. The Romans destroyed the Second Temple, leaving only the Western Wall standing. The Jews who were not killed or captured were cast out of Jerusalem. From the fourth century AD until the early seventh century, the Jews who remained outside Jerusalem persevered under the rule of the Christian emperor Constantine.

ARABS, CRUSADERS, AND OTTOMAN TURKS

Arabs conquered Jerusalem in 638. They erected Muslim monuments, including the Dome of the Rock and the al-Aqsa Mosque. Initially, the Arabs allowed Jews to live and worship freely in the city as long as they paid taxes on their land. However, tolerance for non-Muslims in the Islamic state gradually decreased, and many Jews converted to Islam or fled the country. The Seljuk Turks, a ruling family of the Sunni branch of Islam Turks, captured Jerusalem in 1071, ending Arab rule. The Arabs recovered the city in 1098, and then lost it to Christian crusaders in 1099.

The crusaders were determined to halt the spread of Islam and get the Holy Land back under Christian control. In 1100, they founded the Latin Kingdom of Jerusalem. Most Jews and Muslims residing in the city were violently attacked and murdered, and some were sold into slavery. Muslim sultan Saladin mostly defeated the crusaders in 1187, although a more decisive victory came in 1291 when the Muslim Mamluks, a Turkish military class of slave soldiers, took over. Palestine

THE EXODUS

The Exodus is the biblical story of the Jews' journey from Egypt back to Israel. According to the biblical book of Exodus, God had to cast several plagues on the Egyptians to convince the pharaoh to let the Israelites go. Following a plague killing all Egyptian firstborn children, Moses was allowed to lead the Israelites out of Egypt. As the Bible tells it, when the Egyptians came for the Israelites, God gave Moses power to part the sea. After the Israelites safely crossed the sea, the Egyptians drowned—an occurrence the Israelites attributed to God. Then, the Israelites wandered in the Sinai Desert for 40 years and were able to survive. Christians and Jews believe God provided the Israelites with food and water and that God spoke to Moses atop Mount Sinai and gave him a series of commandments and laws by which the Israelites were to live. These ancient laws, written in the Torah, still govern the lives of religious Jews today.

fell into poverty and ruin under Mamluk rule until the Ottoman Turks, another powerful Muslim Turkish dynasty, conquered it in 1516.

The Holy Land remained under Ottoman rule for four centuries. At the beginning of this period, the small Jewish community remaining in Palestine—mainly in Jerusalem, Nablus, Hebron, Safed, Gaza, and the small towns of Galilee—prospered. But by the end of the eighteenth century, neglectful rulers had allowed the country to fall into disrepair and living conditions were poor. French general Napoléon Bonaparte's activities in the Middle East at the beginning of the nineteenth century led to increased Western influence in Palestine. This shift marginally improved the lives of Jews in the region.

ZIONISM AND WAR

Throughout the nineteenth century, as in many times past, Jews outside Palestine were suffering from varying degrees of oppression and discrimination. An attitude of anti-Semitism was spreading throughout Europe. In the 1880s, it infected the Russian Empire, and a rash of anti-Semitic riots broke out. Many Jews were killed. This uptick in hostility toward Jews touched off a Jewish movement called Zionism—a wish to establish a homeland and safe haven for Jews. In the early 1880s, Jews from Europe and the Russian Empire

The word *anti-Semitism* was coined in the late 1800s and replaced *judeophobia*.

Muslim leader Saladin

began trickling into the region. The following decade, in 1896, Austrian journalist Theodor Herzl launched Political Zionism, proposing a Jewish state be created as a political resolution to the problem of anti-Semitism. It would also give Jews a secular identity. Between 1880 and the beginning of World War I in 1914, the number of Jews in Palestine increased from approximately 25,000 to approximately 85,000.[1]

During the war, the growing population of Jews vied with approximately 600,000 Arabs for control of the region that would become Palestine. Britain also had designs on the region. After the war ended in 1918 and the Ottoman Empire was defeated, the European Allies' interests guided their decisions in dividing the empire. Great Britain took over the region that is now Israel and named it Palestine. The British wanted the area to protect their interests in the Suez Canal, which connects the Red and Mediterranean Seas and is an important shipping route between Europe and Asia that allows traders to bypass Africa. They also wanted a staging area to provide supplies to India, the prize possession of the British Empire. Rather than choosing sides between Jews and Arabs, the British supported the presence of both communities in Palestine. The British acknowledged the Jews' right to return to their ancestral homeland but also vowed to protect the rights of the Arab majority. Each community was granted the right to self-government. The Jewish community was led by Zionist David Ben-Gurion.

Neither Arabs nor Jews were thrilled about having to share the land each side felt was rightfully theirs, but Jews were one step closer to

Zionists gathered in the Palestinian desert in 1909 to choose land to build on and settle. Today, the area is Tel Aviv.

establishing a Jewish state, and Jewish immigration to Palestine continued during this period. The growing Jewish population increased tension between Jews and Arabs. Violence escalated frequently. Britain searched for a peaceful resolution, but to no avail. By the time World War II began in 1939, the British had imposed limitations on Jewish immigration to minimize further conflict.

During World War II (1939–1945), Adolf Hitler's German Nazi Party carried out a genocidal campaign against European Jews. The Nazis systematically murdered approximately 6 million of the 10 million European Jews in death camps.[2] Many survivors of this horror, called

the Holocaust, sought refuge in Palestine, but the British refused to let them in.

Palestinian Jews expressed their outrage vocally and, at times, violently. When diplomatic negotiations with Britain failed, they appealed to the United States for help and welcomed Jewish immigrants into the country illegally. In 1947, Britain asked the United Nations (UN) to help. The UN decided the best solution would be to split Palestine into two states. Approximately half the land would belong to the Jews, half would belong to the Arabs, and Jerusalem would remain under international control.

INDEPENDENCE AND TURMOIL

The Jews accepted the UN's decision. Ben-Gurion declared the independence of the Jewish State of Israel on May 14, 1948. The Arabs had not accepted the UN's plan. After the British withdrew from the area on May 15, armies from surrounding Arab states invaded Israel. The War of Independence lasted until 1949, and Israel prevailed. After establishing armistice, or peace, agreements with its neighbors, Israel had gained significantly more land than the UN had allocated. In addition, per the agreements, Egypt took over the management of an adjacent Palestinian territory called the Gaza Strip, and Jordan oversaw the West

David Ben-Gurion helped found Israel.

Bank—the Palestinian land west of the Jordan River. Hundreds of thousands of Arabs fled the country.

David Ben-Gurion served as Israel's prime minister from 1948 to 1953 and from 1955 to 1963.

With help from abroad, Israel was able to recover from the war, support its immigrant population, and continue its development. Still, the country's Arab neighbors remained hostile. Israel retaliated, and conflict escalated. By the mid-1950s, Egypt had become Israel's primary target. The Egyptians had cut off Israel from important trade routes, including the Suez Canal and the Strait of Tiran. In 1956, Israel teamed with Britain and France in a campaign to invade Egypt's Sinai Peninsula and regain access to these routes. Israeli forces triumphed, though the United States pressured Israel to withdraw from the Sinai Peninsula the following year. UN forces helped keep the peace between the two countries for the next decade.

WAR AND PEACE

In 1967, renewed conflict between Israel and Egypt, Syria, and Jordan culminated in the Six-Day War, which was fought June 5–10. Israel was victorious on all fronts, seizing the Gaza Strip and Sinai Peninsula from Egypt, the West Bank and East Jerusalem from Jordan, and the Golan Heights from Syria. Israelis hoped these occupied territories would give them leverage in negotiations for peace. But this was not to be. After a brief period of peace, Israel's neighbors continued their assault, and Israel struck back. The United States negotiated a tenuous cease-fire in 1970.

In 1973, Egypt and Syria launched a surprise attack on Israel on the Jewish holiday Yom Kippur. Israel managed to maintain its territories, but the military suffered heavy casualties and a blow to its ego, and the country's economy and general morale downturned severely. The war also cost Israel most of its allies. Despite the fact that Israel had not started the war, more and more of its allies found fault with Israel's actions against the Arabs. During the late 1970s, Israel and Egypt took steps to resolve their long-standing conflict. In 1979, Israel agreed to return the Sinai Peninsula to Egypt in exchange for peace. In addition, the countries agreed to diplomatically discuss the question of autonomy for Palestinian Arabs, who were living under Israel's government.

THE PALESTINE LIBERATION ORGANIZATION AND THE INTIFADA

Meanwhile, Israel was under threat from the Palestine Liberation Organization (PLO) forces gathering strength in Lebanon. The PLO—which was fighting for Palestinian interests—had launched several terrorist attacks on Israel, including an assassination attempt on Israel's ambassador to Britain. Israel retaliated in 1982, waging a controversial war against the PLO in southern Lebanon. The United States intervened to negotiate peace.

Even as Israel withdrew from Lebanon, more and more Israeli families were settling in the West Bank and the Gaza Strip. This angered Palestinian residents and led to riots in those territories at the end of

THE PLO AND HAMAS

Several Palestinian groups have had a primary goal of establishing an independent Palestinian state. The PLO was established in 1964 with the goal of representing Palestinians. The organization merged several Palestinian groups, the largest of which was Fatah, led by Yasser Arafat. From the late 1960s to the early 1990s, the PLO launched constant attacks on Israel. Neither the PLO nor Israel recognized the other as a valid entity until the peace process was initiated in the 1990s.

Hamas, or the Islamic Resistance Movement, was formed in 1987 by like-minded groups within the Muslim Brotherhood and the PLO. These groups believed Palestine belonged solely to Muslims. They wanted to start a holy war to take over Israel. Since its inception, Hamas's violent tactics have threatened the safety of Israeli citizens.

1987. The Arab uprising was called the intifada, which means "the act of shaking off."[3] For several months—into 1988—young Palestinians and Israeli soldiers fought each other in the streets.

HOPE FOR PEACE

At the end of 1988, PLO leader Yasser Arafat, who was also the leader of a Palestinian group called Fatah, made the surprising declaration that his organization acknowledged Israel's right to exist and would stop its terrorist attacks on the country. Arafat had taken the first step toward peace, but Israel was not yet ready to negotiate with the PLO. After the Persian Gulf War (1990–1991), Israel agreed to begin peace talks with Lebanon, Syria, and Jordan as well as the Palestinians. However, the secret negotiations

between Israel and the PLO in Oslo, Norway, are what yielded real progress toward peace.

The Oslo Accords of 1993 laid the foundation for future peaceful relations between Israelis and their Palestinian neighbors. This agreement outlined Israel's intention to grant autonomy to Palestinians in the Gaza Strip and Jericho and to continue to negotiate with the PLO. In 1995, Israel promised in a second agreement to gradually withdraw from other areas of the West Bank. By this time, Israel had also signed a peace treaty with Jordan, although Syria remained uncooperative. The Middle East slowly progressed toward a fragile peace.

Yasser Arafat

Palestinians and Israelis threatened this peace. Hamas, a Palestinian Islamic group opposed to the Oslo Accords, launched several attacks on Israeli civilians during the 1990s. The PLO failed to suppress these attacks. In 1995, an ultraorthodox Jew assassinated Israel's prime minister, Yitzhak Rabin, in an attempt to halt the peace process. Despite these setbacks, Israel continued to follow through on its agreements with the PLO. In January 1996, Arafat was elected head of the Palestinian Authority (PA), the governing body of Palestinians in the West Bank and the Gaza Strip.

By 1997, tension had flared between Israelis and Palestinians, and relations between the Israeli government and the Fatah-dominated PA had slid back into mutual distrust. Efforts toward resolving the conflict in the following years led nowhere, and in 2000, a second intifada broke out. Violence between Israelis and Palestinians continued until 2004, when Arafat's death led to renewed negotiations. A cease-fire was attained in 2005 after Israel agreed to evacuate Jewish residents from the West Bank and the Gaza Strip according to the US Roadmap to Peace. This peace gave way in 2007 when, after violent skirmishes between Hamas and Fatah forces in the region, Hamas took over the Gaza Strip and

THE SECURITY FENCE

In response to ongoing terrorism, Israel began constructing a security barrier between Israel and the West Bank in 2002. Some Israelis opposed the idea of a security fence, arguing it would be expensive, ineffective, and would incite conflict rather than stop it. However, with the support of more than 83 percent of Israelis, construction continued.[4] The security fence has deterred Palestinian attacks.

An Israeli woman protested at the border to the Gaza Strip in 2006—the issue remains unresolved.

continued its attacks on Israel. Conflict between Israel and Hamas escalated between 2008 and 2009. More than 1,000 people were killed. Today, Israel continues to walk the fine line between defending itself and seeking peace with its neighbors.

CHAPTER 5

PEOPLE: A NATION OF IMMIGRANTS

In 1948, the fledgling State of Israel was home to approximately 872,000 people.[1] Jewish immigrants streamed into the country they claimed as their homeland, while people of other backgrounds saw an opportunity to make a new life in Israel. The population of the tiny country boomed. Today, Israel is crowded with more than 7.5 million people of richly varied cultures, languages, races, and religions.[2]

More than 76 percent of Israelis are Jewish.[3] This group is a diverse mixture of native-born Jews and those who have come from countries across Europe, Africa, Asia, and the Americas. Israel's eclectic Jewish community comprises a broad spectrum of customs, beliefs, and languages.

Judaism is the oldest surviving monotheistic religion.

Jewish refugees from Europe looked to the shore as they neared Palestine by boat in 1946.

YOU SAY IT!

English	Hebrew	Arabic
Hello	Shalom (shah-LOHM)	Salaamu alaikum (sah-LAH-moo ah-LAY-koom)
Good-bye	Shalom (shah-LOHM)	Ma'as salaama (MAH-ahs sah-LAH-mah)
Please	Bevakasha (bay-vah-kah-SHAH)	Min fadlik (f.) (mihn FAHD-lihk) Min fadlak (m.) (mihn FAHD-lahk)
Thank you	Toda (toh-DAH)	Shokran (shohk-rahn)
Yes	Ken (kehn)	Naam (nahm)
No	Lo (loh)	La (lah)
How are you?	Ma shlomekh? (f.) (mah shloh-MAYKH) Ma shlomkha? (m.) (mah-shlohm-KHAH)	Kaif halik? (f.) (kayf HAH-lihk) Kaif halak? (m.) (kayf HAH-lahk)

f. = feminine; m. = masculine

The remainder of Israel's population is mostly Arab. Many are Muslim; others are Christian or Druze. Most speak Arabic; some speak Hebrew. Most live in cities; some range across the Negev. Arabs and Jews do not always see eye to eye, and the country they share is more vibrant for their differences.

JEWS

Jews in Israel are united by a shared religion, a similar cultural heritage, and the ancient Hebrew language. They are descendants of the founders of Judaism or believers in its tenets, or beliefs. In general, Jews believe in one god who is the creator and ruler of all that exists. They believe they have an especially close relationship with God, who has instructed them to abide by certain laws. These laws are written in the Torah, the first five books of the Hebrew Bible. Additionally, Jews believe God will someday bring about universal peace, justice, and obedience to God's will.

In many ways, Jews are more different than they are alike. They have grouped themselves into separate communities based on cultural differences and varying degrees of adherence to scripture. The two main culturally distinct groups are the Ashkenazim and the Sephardim. The Ashkenazim come from Europe and speak Hebrew, Yiddish, or their native European languages. The Sephardim come from Spain, Portugal, North Africa, and Turkey. Many Sephardim speak Ladino, an old form of Spanish mixed with Hebrew. These two groups have different ritual practices, and each has its own chief rabbi. The Oriental Jews are a third cultural group. Coming primarily from the Middle East, many Oriental

KIBBUTZIM AND MOSHAVIM

Approximately 10 percent of Jews live in rural communities.[4] Of these, approximately half live in communal settlements called kibbutzim and moshavim.[5] On a kibbutz, all members work to maintain a common business, which is usually related to farming. All money, property, and services are shared equally among members, and decisions are made by majority vote. On many kibbutzim, children are also collectively raised and cared for.

Moshavim are similar to kibbutzim but less extreme in their collectivity. On a moshav, children live with and are raised by their parents, and households are privately owned. Each household usually has its own plot to farm, and the entire moshav cooperates in buying goods and selling produce. On some moshavim, the land is farmed collectively.

Jews speak Arabic or a mixture of Arabic and Hebrew. Other substantial groups include Russian Jews, who immigrated in large numbers from the former Soviet Union in the 1990s, and Ethiopian Jews, most of whom immigrated between 1980 and 1992.

Jews are further divided into those who strictly adhere to Jewish law and those who do not. Many within the latter group are secular—they do not actively practice Judaism. Nonorthodox Jews are actively religious but do not strictly follow Jewish law. Orthodox Jews scrupulously observe the laws written in the Torah. Even so, Orthodox Jews are split into ultraorthodox, or *Haredi*, and neoorthodox. Ultraorthodox Jews maintain traditional dress and isolate themselves from secular influences; neoorthodox Jews observe the laws while fully integrating into modern society. From ultraorthodox to secular, the majority of Jews live in cities.

ARABS

Arabs are an equally diverse ethnic group. The Arabs who lived in the region that became Palestine were primarily farmers, and many farmed land owned by someone higher in the social hierarchy. These Arabs had a class-based social structure, with the highest social class descended from the Prophet Muhammad. Most Arabs living in Israel today are Muslim, or followers of Islam. Like Jews, Muslims believe in one god: Allah. Muslims must surrender to the will of Allah, which they believe was revealed to Muhammad and is recorded in the Koran. To demonstrate their submission to Allah, Muslims practice the five pillars of Islam. These include rules for professing one's faith, praying, giving money to the poor, fasting, and making a pilgrimage to Mecca, Saudi Arabia, considered the center of Islam. Both Sunni and Shia Muslims live in Israel. The two branches of Islam hold different beliefs about Muhammad's successors. Sunni Muslims have the greater influence in Israel.

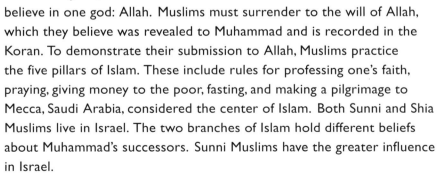

THE AGE OF ISRAEL'S POPULATION[6]

65+ years: 10.3%

0–14 years: 27.5%

15–64 years: 62.2%

Prayer is an important practice for Muslims.

Approximately 10 percent of Arabs in Israel are Bedouin.[7] These pastoral people are virtually all Muslims. Those who maintain a traditional lifestyle move from place to place with their sheep, goats, or camels, living in tents alongside their herds. Many Bedouin have given up their nomadic existence in favor of a more settled lifestyle. Most Israeli Bedouin live in the Negev. Other Bedouin communities have developed in northern and central Israel.

Approximately 2 percent of Israelis are Christian, and they are mostly Arab.[8] Christians believe in one god and that Jesus Christ is

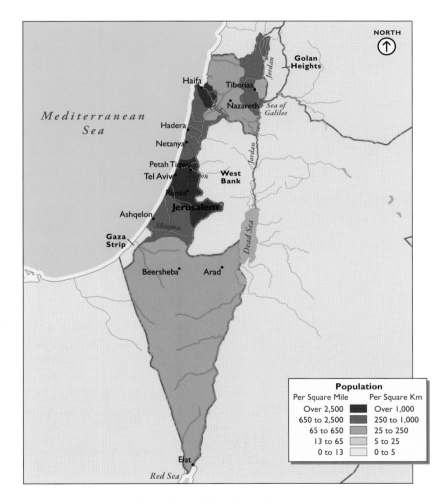

NORTH
↑

Golan
Heights

Haifa
Tiberias
Nazareth

*Mediterranean
Sea*

Hadera

Netanya

Petah Tiqwa
Tel Aviv
Yarqon

West
Bank

Ramla

Jerusalem

Ashqelon

Gaza
Strip

Shiqma

Beersheba
Arad

Elat

Red Sea

Jordan

*Sea of
Galilee*

Jordan

Dead Sea

Population

Per Square Mile		Per Square Km
Over 2,500		Over 1,000
650 to 2,500		250 to 1,000
65 to 650		25 to 250
13 to 65		5 to 25
0 to 13		0 to 5

Population Density of Israel

the son of God. According to Christian belief, God sent Jesus to Earth. Following his crucifixion and death, Jesus rose from the dead. Christians believe his death atoned for the sins of humankind. The many branches of Christianity present in Israel include Greek Catholic, Greek Orthodox, Roman Catholic, and a few Protestant denominations.

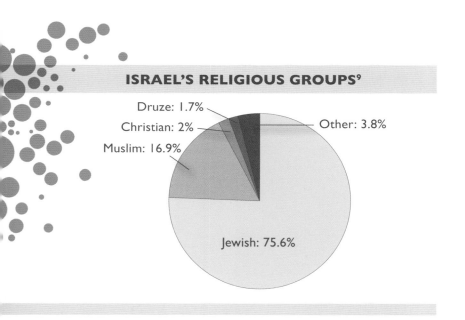

ISRAEL'S RELIGIOUS GROUPS⁹

Druze: 1.7%
Christian: 2%
Muslim: 16.9%
Other: 3.8%
Jewish: 75.6%

A slightly smaller and much more mysterious Arab group is the Druze. Their monotheistic religion is cloaked in secrecy, even from many of its followers. Knowledge of the Druze faith is passed down through a select group of initiates. Israel's close-knit Druze community is centered in the rural north.

MINORITY ETHNIC GROUPS

Smaller minority ethnic groups in Israel include African Hebrew Israelites, Circassians,

Israelis in Isfiya, a Druze village, celebrate an annual religious festival.

Armenians, Baha'is, and foreign workers. African Hebrew Israelites, an African-American religious group founded in Chicago, Illinois, believe they descend from the ancient Israelites. Thousands of African Hebrew Israelites have moved from the Americas and developed their own communities in southern Israel.

The Circassians are a Caucasian Sunni Muslim people. They speak Circassian, as well as Arabic and Hebrew. They keep their culture and traditions alive in villages in the Galilee region of northern Israel.

Approximately 1,000 Armenians live in Jerusalem. Approximately half live in the Armenian Quarter of Jerusalem's Old City.[10] They are one

ETHIOPIAN JEWS

The ancestors of Ethiopian Jews held onto their faith when Christians gained control of Ethiopia in the fourth century and tried to force Jews to convert. Several centuries later, Ethiopian Jews rose to power under new rule. But after approximately 350 years, Christians reclaimed Ethiopia, and Jews were savagely persecuted. This oppression continued into the twentieth century. Various Jewish groups offered aid and assisted with travel to Israel. In the late 1970s, war broke out in Ethiopia. Between 1980 and 1992, approximately 45,000 Ethiopian Jews fled their native land and—with the help of Israeli organizations—made their way to Israel.[12] Many Ethiopian Jewish families were separated in the process, and they faced the added challenges of learning Hebrew and integrating into Israeli culture. Israel also struggled to absorb the large numbers of immigrants. However, the Israeli government currently supports the immigration of Ethiopian Jews to Israel.

of the largest non-Arab Christian groups in the area. In Haifa, a small number of Baha'is live near the religion's headquarters on Mount Carmel. And foreign workers from various countries in Europe, Asia—including India—and Africa fill many low-paying jobs in Israel. Since 2005, approximately 60,000 Africans have entered the country illegally.[11] Israel's diverse groups are learning to navigate each other's differences to live together simply as fellow Israelis.

Ethiopian Jews pray during a holiday celebration.

CHAPTER 6

CULTURE: SHAPED BY DIFFERENCES

Israel's thousands of immigrants brought with them strands of their native culture: sacred rituals, beloved music, traditional crafts, lively dances, delicious foods, and familiar languages. Over time, these colorful strands have twisted together to lend strength and beauty to a nation shaped by differences. Israelis' shared history and experiences of war, exile, and discrimination also bind them together and strongly influence their culture.

Modern Hebrew is the only spoken language successfully revived from a written language.

LANGUAGE AND LITERATURE

The revival of Hebrew as a spoken language in Israel has been important in giving Jewish immigrants a sense of unity.

Part of the Israel Museum, the Shrine of the Book is home to the Dead Sea Scrolls, ancient writings of the Hebrew Bible.

The most prominent early Hebrew writer in Israel was Shmuel Yosef Agnon (1888–1970). His novels and short stories explored the struggles of the Jewish people and tensions arising from cultural and religious differences. *Tmol shilshom*, published in 1945 and translated in English as *Only Yesterday*, is his most famous work. Agnon was awarded the Nobel Prize for Literature in 1966.

Poet Haim Nahman Bialik (1873–1934) was celebrated for using the Hebrew language in new ways. His powerful verses, which trace both religious and political themes, strongly resonated with the Jewish people. Bialik moved to Palestine in 1924, a decade before his death. His former home in Tel Aviv has become a national landmark in Israel.

Authors of modern Hebrew literature, written in the late 1900s and early 2000s, tend to use less formal language than their predecessors. Israeli poet Yehuda Amichai is well known and beloved for making his poems accessible through everyday language. Current writers often

THE ISRAEL MUSEUM

The Israel Museum in Jerusalem is the nation's largest museum. The building's multiple wings are devoted to archaeology, fine arts, Jewish culture, and youth education. The Shrine of the Book is also part of the museum. Its onion-shaped dome hovers protectively over the Dead Sea Scrolls. People first discovered portions of these important Hebrew manuscripts in 1947, and more fragments were discovered over the next decade, until 1965. The manuscripts were located in jars near the Dead Sea and are approximately 2,000 years old. The Shrine of the Book was modeled after the lids of the jars in which the first scrolls were found.

explore Israeli national identity and modern Jewish issues. Some write about war, conflict, or memories of the Holocaust. Others write about everyday life and relationships or what life is like on kibbutzim.

Arabic literature has also flourished in Israel. Arab writer Emile Habibi (1922–1996) grew up in Haifa. He wrote about the inner turmoil experienced by many Palestinians during the Arab-Israeli conflict, and his novels became popular throughout the Middle East. Habibi was awarded the Israel Prize for Arabic literature in 1992.

Other Arab authors, such as Sayed Kashua, write in Hebrew. The passionate political poetry of Mahmoud Darwish and works of other Arab Israeli writers are increasingly taught in Israel's public schools.

MUSIC AND DANCE

Israel has a vibrant music scene. While religious folk songs once strengthened the bond between Jews, rock, pop, and Middle Eastern music have since become more popular. Melodic ballads sung by pop musicians such as Rami Kleinstein and Rita have especially widespread appeal. Many new Israeli singers have gained a following through televised song contests similar to the popular US program *American Idol*.

Musika mizrahit is the catchy sound track to Israel's cultural diversity. This style of music blends Middle Eastern, Mediterranean, and Western influences. It was rarely played on public airwaves until the 1990s and has become a mainstream and celebrated part of Israel's music scene. Jazz and classical music are also popular in Israel. Each year, jazz musicians from around the world gather in Elat for four days at the Red Sea Jazz Festival. The Israel Philharmonic Orchestra has achieved international renown through its performances of classical works across the globe. Its famously talented musicians include violinist Itzhak Perlman and pianist Daniel Barenboim.

Folk dances accompany the traditional musical styles of each of Israel's ethnic groups. African, European, Russian, Indian, and Middle Eastern folk dances have kept traditions alive in a new land. They have influenced folk dances specific to Israel, which began developing in the 1940s to help establish a national identity. The hora is one of the most popular folk dances. Dancers join hands and form a circle, executing fancy footwork in time with upbeat Israeli folk music. Contemporary dance and ballet have also flourished in Israel, with several dance companies—such as the Kibbutz Contemporary Dance Company and the Israel Ballet—providing opportunities for young dancers.

FILM AND THEATER

Israeli cinema has its roots in the 1900s, when films such as *This Is the Land* (1935) were used to promote the Zionist movement. After World War II, Jewish filmmakers focused on the Holocaust. This haunting subject gave way to the more immediate concerns of the Arab-Israeli conflict after Israel's independence. Films of this period—including Israel's first feature film, *Hill 24 Doesn't Answer* (1955)—often romanticized the Israeli warrior.

Itzhak Perlman

A poster for the Israeli film *Waltz with Bashir*

In the 1960s, experimental films and comedies emerged as an alternative for battle-weary audiences. *Bourekas* comedies poked fun at the prejudices and stereotypes of Ashkenazic and Oriental Jews. The Bourekas film *Sallah* (1964), the hero of which was an Oriental Jew, was the first Israeli film to receive an Academy Award nomination. Amidst the political turmoil of the 1970s and 1980s, Israeli filmmakers once again trained their lenses on war and conflict. Instead of featuring glorified Israeli hero-warriors, films tended to depict the miseries of war in gritty realism. Filmmakers portrayed Israeli soldiers and Holocaust survivors as multidimensional human beings traumatized by their experiences.

After a wave of films in the late 1980s and 1990s that avoided politics, cinema underwent a renaissance in the twenty-first century. Contemporary Israeli films explore the country's cultural diversity in detail. Many of them tell the stories of minority groups not previously represented in film. Israeli films are beginning to make an impression abroad. *Waltz with Bashir* (2008) achieved international success, and Israeli filmmakers are constantly adding to their collection of prestigious awards.

Themes in Israeli theater closely mirror those expressed in film. Nationalistic plays about early war victories were followed by a movement toward surrealism and escapism, exemplified by plays such as Nissim Aloni's *The King's New Clothes* (1961). Politics gradually crept back into theater, and by the 1980s, the stage had become a platform for protesters. Today, theater in Israel has become more focused on pure entertainment. Many plays are adapted from abroad. Most original Israeli plays are written and performed in Hebrew, although Beit HaGeffen Theater in Haifa produces Arabic plays.

VISUAL ART AND ARCHITECTURE

The founding of the Bezalel School of Arts and Crafts—now the Bezalel Academy of Arts and Design—in Jerusalem in 1906 marked the beginning of modern Israeli art. Israeli culture has been celebrated in colorful abstract paintings such as Yehezkel Streichman's *Ein Hod* (1956) and criticized with haunting sculptures, including Igael Tumarkin's *He Walked in the Fields* (1967). War and conflict are continually explored through art, though visual art can also be a welcome escape from the turbulence of Israel's political climate. Many contemporary artists avoid political commentary and instead seek to transport viewers through the beauty of their work.

Israeli architecture is a unique mixture of ancient and modern. Jerusalem's Old City preserves the ancient in its limestone facings and archways, Byzantine churches, and elaborate mosques. Tel Aviv is known for its Bauhaus architecture, which is characterized by geometric shapes and asymmetrical lines. Most Bauhaus structures in Israel are white and have small windows. Glass skyscrapers and other modern structures also grace Tel Aviv's skyline.

SPORTS AND RECREATION

Israel has become a nation of sports fans. Once aligned with political parties, Israeli sports teams now draw regional fans regardless of political alliance. Israelis love to cheer on their favorite soccer teams. Beitar Jerusalem, Hapoel Tel Aviv, and Maccabi Haifa are the major teams. Israelis are also passionate about basketball, and the Maccabi Tel Aviv team has done particularly well internationally. Tennis and handball are other popular sports. Arabs and Israelis play side by side on most sports teams.

Bauhaus architecture is common in Tel Aviv.

With the country's long, inviting Mediterranean coast, Israelis enjoy a variety of water sports. Swimming, surfing, windsurfing, sailing, and scuba diving are popular activities in the country's warm seas. Since Israel entered the Olympic Games in 1952, most of the country's medals have been in water sports. The rest have been in martial arts. Every four years, Israel hosts the Jewish version of the Olympic Games. The Maccabiah Games draw thousands of Jewish athletes from around the world.

Israelis participate in indoor activities as well. Many play chess or backgammon. Watching television is another favorite pastime, with most Israelis tuning in for news, reality programs, or comedies. Many Israeli television shows are adapted from programs that are popular abroad. Citizens are also fond of surfing the Internet. Most Israeli Web sites are in Hebrew or English.

FOOD AND DRINK

Israeli cuisine is shaped by religious and cultural diversity. The majority of Israeli Jews keep kosher, eating only those foods allowed by Jewish law. Religious Jews avoid pork and shellfish, and they do not eat meat and dairy in the same meal. Many other foods must be prepared in accordance with strict rules. Similarly, religious Muslims do not eat pork or drink alcohol. Animals that are not correctly slaughtered and blessed are also forbidden to Muslims.

Traditional Jewish foods include latkes, or potato pancakes; matzo, or unleavened bread; gefilte fish patties; *cholent*, or stews; and honeyed sweets. Middle Eastern foods such as chickpea-based falafel and hummus are popular. Lamb is a favorite meat often served skewered on kabobs or shredded. Asian and Mediterranean dishes are widely

Devout Jewish families eat meat and dairy from separate sets of dishes.

Players from the Maccabi Haifa soccer team posed in 2011.

enjoyed, and pizza is a common fast-food choice. Israelis have easy access to fresh produce, meat, and dairy year-round. Strong coffee is a necessity for most Israelis, and many enjoy a glass of kosher wine from time to time. On hot days, many enjoy *limonana*, lemonade with crushed mint leaves.

HOLIDAYS AND FESTIVALS

Most holidays in Israel are religious, and the dates often vary with religious calendars. Rosh Hashanah, the Jewish New Year, is celebrated in the fall. Some families attend synagogue, or temple, and others enjoy beachside picnics. Eating foods dipped in honey is a traditional way of ensuring the new year will be sweet. Yom Kippur is the holiest day of the Jewish calendar. All businesses close while religious Jews fast and pray. Hanukkah spans eight days in December. Jewish families traditionally light menorahs, eat fried foods, and exchange small gifts. During Passover in the spring, Jewish families eat matzo and celebrate their ancestors' journey from Egypt back to the Promised Land.

The Jewish calendar is based on the moon.

For Israeli Muslims, the holy month of Ramadan is a time of introspection. Muslims pray, study the Koran, and fast between sunrise and sunset. Families gather each evening to break their fast

Falafels, hummus, and pita bread are staples in Middle Eastern cuisine.

THE SABBATH

The Jewish Shabbat, or holy day of rest, begins at sundown Friday and lasts until nightfall Saturday. During Shabbat, religious Jews are not allowed to work, which includes cooking, traveling, writing, and even answering the phone. To avoid working on Shabbat, Jewish families prepare meals ahead of time and either slow-cook or reheat the food. Many Jews also attend synagogue on Shabbat.

Christians traditionally honor their Sabbath on Sunday by attending church and avoiding business transactions. Friday is a holy day for Muslims, and many gather at mosques to pray. Israelis typically work from Sunday through Thursday to accommodate Jewish and Muslim rituals.

together. A three-day feast called Eid al-Fitr marks the end of Ramadan. During Eid al-Adha, the Festival of Sacrifice, Muslim families slaughter an animal and give some of the meat to the poor. Christian holidays, including Easter and Christmas, are celebrated differently according to the traditions of each Christian group. Many Israelis turn out to enjoy the parades and fireworks of Independence Day, which falls in April or May, according to the Jewish calendar. Other national holidays honor Holocaust victims and soldiers who died fighting for Israel.

Muslim youth perform in Jerusalem during the month of Ramadan in celebration of a break in the fasting.

CHAPTER 7
POLITICS: A JEWISH DEMOCRACY

Like most things in Israel, the country's politics are a synthesis of the traditional and the progressive. Israel is both a democratic state and a Jewish one, with religious tradition serving as a counterpoint to modern ideals. Ancient battles have also been carried into the present. The Israeli-Palestinian conflict is never far from the minds of Israeli citizens or elected officials.

The twenty-first century has failed to bring Israel's political upheaval to an end. Peace talks between the Israeli government and the PLO resumed in 2010 only to be stalled weeks later when Israel lifted a ban on Jewish settlements in the West Bank. In 2011, a wave of uprisings in the Middle East and questionable decisions by Israeli soldiers abroad resulted in increased animosity toward Israel. Political activists also filled Israel's streets that summer, protesting inequality in all its forms. Although the

A menorah stands tall in front of Israel's parliament building as a reminder of the nation's Jewish tradition.

Palestinian Hamas and Fatah groups reconciled in 2011, the PA and the Israeli government have yet to follow suit. A two-state solution, which would grant both Palestinians and Israelis independent states within Palestine, holds promise for peace. A number of issues, including the role of Hamas in the PA and the status of Jewish settlements in Palestinian territories, must be resolved before an agreement can be reached.

The Israeli government strives to achieve balance in the midst of this instability. Israel is a democratic country in which all Israelis 18 years and older can participate in electing officials to represent them. The Israeli government consists of three branches: legislative, executive, and judicial.

STRUCTURE OF THE GOVERNMENT OF ISRAEL

Executive Branch	Legislative Branch	Judicial Branch
President (head of state) Prime minister (head of government) Cabinet	Knesset (120 members, all representatives of the entire nation elected by the people)	Supreme Court District courts Magistrate's courts Religious and military tribunals

THE LEGISLATIVE BRANCH

The Knesset is Israel's legislative, or lawmaking, body. Its 120 members are elected to four-year terms, although elections have historically happened more frequently than every four years. Nationwide elections are held, with political parties submitting lists of candidates for the Knesset. Each party lists its candidates in order of priority: the first name on the list is the party's candidate for prime minister. Citizens vote for the party whose list they prefer. Each party with at least 2 percent of the vote wins seats in the Knesset in proportion to the number of votes, and the candidates listed first take the seats. In 2009, 12 parties won seats in the Knesset.[1] Kadima won the most, with 28 seats.[2] The Jewish Home, New Movement-Meretz, and Balad Parties each won three seats, the fewest of all the parties.[3]

> **Any Israeli at least 21 years old is eligible to run for the Knesset.**

THE EXECUTIVE BRANCH

Israel's executive branch includes the president, the prime minister, and the prime minister's cabinet. The Knesset elects Israel's president to serve one seven-year term. The president's role as head of state is largely ceremonial. However, he or she appoints judges, Supreme Court justices, and other important officials. Shimon Peres was elected president in 2007.

Shimon Peres, Israel's president

Israel's president also nominates the prime minister, who must then be approved by the Knesset. The president may nominate the candidate nominated by the party with the most Knesset seats or another person. The prime minister serves as head of government and leader of the country. The president traditionally chooses the party leader supported by the majority of Knesset members for the post. Since Israel's election process makes it difficult for any single political party to achieve a majority of Knesset seats, coalition governments are the norm. The prime minister is responsible for forming a coalition of parties that generally agree on how the country should be run. He or she must also choose the cabinet, which decides government policies and advises the prime minister. Powerful positions in the cabinet are often given to nonleading parties in exchange for joining the coalition. Benjamin Netanyahu became Israel's prime minister in 2009.

THE JUDICIAL BRANCH

Israel's judicial branch, or justice system, includes the country's courts and is independent from the other two branches of the government. The Supreme Court is the highest court. Its ten justices are appointed by the president with the help of the Israeli Judicial Committee. The Supreme Court delivers the final ruling on cases appealed to it, tries cases that do not fall under the jurisdiction, or authority, of lower courts, and determines the constitutionality of laws and other government actions.

Lower courts include district courts, magistrate's courts, and religious and military tribunals. The Israeli Judicial Committee appoints

THE ISRAELI FLAG

Israel's flag is white with a blue six-pointed star in the center and blue horizontal bands above and below. The star, commonly known as the Star of David, is a symbol of Judaism. The flag's design is also similar in appearance to the traditional Jewish prayer shawl. Israel officially adopted this flag in 1948, approximately six months after declaring its independence.

judges for these courts. The six district courts rule on severe criminal and civil cases. The 29 magistrate's courts address minor cases. Religious tribunals generally deal with personal and family matters such as marriage. Jews, Muslims, Christians, and Druze each have their own religious courts. Military tribunals deal with offenses committed by Israeli soldiers.

LOCAL GOVERNMENT

Israel is divided into six districts: Northern, Central, Southern, Jerusalem, Haifa, and Tel Aviv. These are further broken down into 15 subdistricts. Municipalities govern the larger towns, including Jerusalem, Haifa, and Tel Aviv. Towns with populations of fewer than 20,000 people are governed by local councils. Regional councils are made up of representatives from each of the small settlements under their jurisdiction.

Israel's flag

THE PA

The PA government has a structure similar to the Israeli government. The Palestinian Legislative Council is the lawmaking body. It has 132 members.[4] Half are representatives of districts, and half are elected through proportional representation of political parties. Like the Israeli government, the PA has both a president and a prime minister. The president is directly elected by the people. He or she appoints the prime minister, and the prime minister assembles a cabinet. After Hamas and Fatah reconciled in 2011, former PA president Mahmoud Abbas was appointed interim prime minister until elections could be held.

Israel's local governments are responsible for providing their communities with basic infrastructure and services, including parks, roads, schools, social services, and utilities. Local elections take place every five years. As in the Knesset, political parties gain seats on councils or municipalities based on proportional representation.

BASIC LAWS

Israel has no written constitution, in part, following what the British had done when in control, but mainly because its leaders have not been able to agree on the extent to which religion should play a role in the government. Instead, the Knesset has passed several Basic Laws. Many define the roles of the three branches of the government; one declares Jerusalem as the nation's capital. They also protect the basic rights and freedoms of Israeli citizens. Together, these laws act like a constitution.

There have been 14 Basic Laws, the first of which was passed in 1958. The most recent of the laws was passed in 2001.

MAJOR POLITICAL PARTIES AND ISSUES

The abundance of political parties in Israel can be both a blessing and a curse. While it ensures that a wide range of views are represented, it can make the government less efficient and less stable. The three major parties in Israel are the Labor Party, Likud, and Kadima.

The Labor Party dominated Israeli politics from 1948 through 1977. Since then, it has lost much of its support. A left-wing party, the Labor Party has traditionally been more willing to negotiate with Palestinians, including sacrificing land for peace. It also supports more generous social benefits than other groups.

"The State of Israel . . . will be based on freedom, justice, and peace as envisaged by the prophets of Israel; it will ensure complete equality of social and political rights to all its inhabitants irrespective of religion, race, or sex; it will guarantee freedom of religion, conscience, language, education, and culture; it will safeguard the Holy Places of all religions; and it will be faithful to the principles of the Charter of the United Nations."[5]

—Declaration of the Establishment of the State of Israel (May 14, 1948)

Likud is the major right-wing nationalist party. Likud members are generally opposed to giving up land to Palestinians and believe Jews have a right to settle in the West Bank and Gaza Strip. The party is also against Palestinian statehood. Prime Minister Netanyahu is the current leader of the Likud Party. Kadima split from Likud in 2005 to become the major centrist party in Israel. Kadima members support the two-state solution and are in favor of withdrawing from Palestinian territories.

Israelis remain divided on a few core political issues. The Palestinian question is constant, and while all Israelis recognize the need for peace with their neighbors, no party has proposed a solution acceptable to the majority of Israelis. Religion is also an issue. Israel's Declaration of the Establishment of the State of Israel, its declaration of independence, established Israel as a Jewish state, and many Israelis would like religion to have more influence on government policy. Others call for the complete separation of religion and state. Whether Israel's coalition governments will be able to resolve these issues, unify Israelis, and achieve peace remains to be seen.

Benjamin Netanyahu, Israel's prime minister

CHAPTER 8
ECONOMICS: A SELF-MADE NATION

Israel has overcome continuous obstacles to create one of the world's strongest economies. The first waves of Jewish immigrants arrived in a dry, barren land. They maximized their scarce water supplies and irrigated their land to make it fertile. Agriculture alone could not support Israel's rapidly growing population, and immigrants contributed greatly to the development of infrastructure and industry. However, the War of Independence crippled Israel's progress. The government was forced to ration food and other materials starting in 1949.

Aid from other nations—particularly the United States—as well as war reparations from Germany helped Israel recover. The economy boomed throughout most of the 1950s and 1960s. In the early 1970s, war again caused a crisis. The 1985 Economic Stabilization Plan quickly stabilized the economy, which then surged into growth and withstood

Israel's currency is the new Israel shekel.

Arab boycotts, ongoing conflict, and recessions. Today, with a per capita gross domestic product of $31,400, Israel is one of the wealthiest countries in the world, and its citizens enjoy one of the highest standards of living.[1]

NATURAL RESOURCES AND INDUSTRY

Israel's primary natural resources are minerals and natural gas. Potash, magnesium, and bromine are mined from the Dead Sea, and copper ore can be found in the valley to the south. The Negev region is rich in phosphates, which are primarily used for making fertilizers.

Oil and natural gas reserves lie beneath the sands of the Negev and along the Mediterranean coast. Since these fossil fuels are not enough to meet Israel's needs, the country imports most of its energy. However, recent natural gas discoveries may help Israel reduce

ISRAEL'S CURRENCY

Israel's currency is the new Israeli shekel, which is divided into 100 agorot. It was adopted in 1985 to replace the old shekel at a rate of 1,000 old shekels to one new Israeli shekel. Israeli banknotes come in denominations of 20, 50, 100, and 200. The fronts of the bills have images of important Israeli figures. The backs display images of culturally important places or events. Israeli coins come in denominations of one, five, and ten new Israeli shekels and one, ten, and 50 agorot.

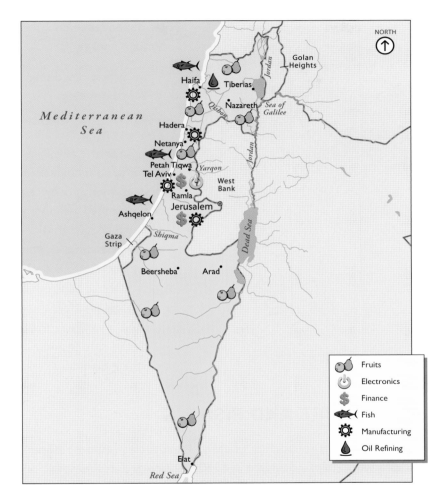

Resources of Israel

Legend:
- Fruits
- Electronics
- Finance
- Fish
- Manufacturing
- Oil Refining

OCCUPATIONS IN ISRAEL[4]

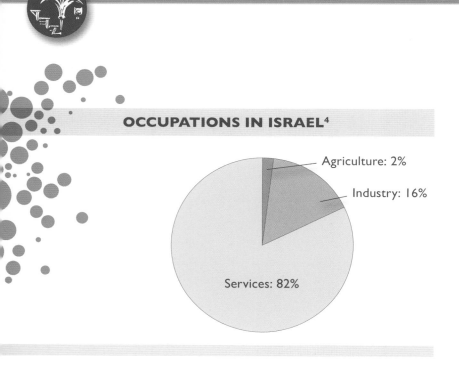

Agriculture: 2%

Industry: 16%

Services: 82%

its dependence on foreign energy.

Technology dominates Israel's industries. The country manufactures a variety of electronics, computer and software systems, communication devices, medical devices, and advanced weaponry. Other manufactured products include chemicals, pharmaceuticals, military equipment, food products, metal, and plastics. Israel is also the world leader in cutting and polishing diamonds.

AGRICULTURE AND FISHING

Agriculture was the foundation of early Israeli society. Almost 20 percent of Israelis worked in agriculture in 1950.[2] Although it accounts for only 2 percent of the country's jobs today, agriculture remains an essential part of Israel's economy.[3]

Oranges are one of Israel's many crops.

Israelis have developed advanced irrigation technologies to conserve as much water as possible while still meeting agricultural needs. The country is known for producing citrus, especially oranges. Cotton, peanuts, and sugar beets are other valuable crops. In addition to producing much of the country's food, Israeli farmers grow a variety of fruits, vegetables, and flowers in greenhouses to export during the off-season. Livestock farmers raise primarily cattle and chickens, and Israel has a successful dairy industry that is helping transform it into the "land flowing with milk and honey" the Hebrew Bible describes.[5]

Fishers cast their nets off Israel's Mediterranean and Red Sea coasts, but with marine life dwindling in these warm seas, they have better luck farther out in the Indian and Atlantic Oceans. Fish farming in inland ponds has also proven successful.

SERVICES AND TOURISM

More than 80 percent of Israelis have service jobs.[6] Many work for the government, which controls banks, power plants, defense manufacturers, and other businesses. Others offer their services in schools, hospitals, office buildings, shops, and restaurants.

Approximately 25 percent of Israelis' income goes to the government as taxes.[8]

Tourism is one of Israel's most important service industries. Although the threat of violence sometimes discourages tourists, Israel welcomed more than 1.5 million visitors in 2010.[7] Jewish pilgrims—as well as many tourists of other faiths—go to pray at the Western Wall. Muslims visit the Dome of the Rock. Christians frequent the Church of the Holy Sepulchre in Jerusalem and the West Bank cities of Nazareth and Bethlehem. Nonreligious destinations include coastal beaches, archaeological sites, and the Dead Sea. Visitors also enjoy bird-watching or immersing themselves in the culture and nightlife of Israel's cities.

IMPORTS AND EXPORTS

With few natural resources, Israel depends heavily on trade and often imports more products than it exports. Imports include raw materials, manufacturing machinery, military equipment, fuels, and food. Surrounding Arab countries prefer not to trade with Israel, so the majority of these products come from the United States, China, and the European Union.

High-tech products such as electronics, aircraft, and pharmaceuticals make up approximately one-third of Israel's exports.[9] Other valuable exports include cut and polished diamonds and agricultural products. Israel also trades services, such as offering hospitality to tourists and investing in other nations' economies. Its primary export partner is the United States, followed by Hong Kong, Belgium, the United Kingdom, India, and China.

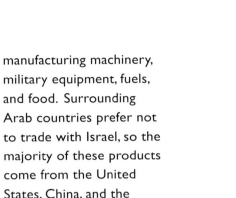

MINING THE DEAD SEA

Miners collect minerals from the Dead Sea using an evaporation pool created at the southern end and separated by a dike. Mineral-rich water is pumped from the Dead Sea into giant evaporating pans. After the water evaporates from the pans, the minerals left behind can be easily harvested for further processing. Salts from the Dead Sea are used and sold for medicinal purposes and for skin care. Unfortunately, the process of mining the Dead Sea also contributes to its decreasing water levels.

INFRASTRUCTURE

Israel's highly developed infrastructure includes the most advanced communications system in the Middle East. There are more mobile phones in use in Israel than there are Israelis. Israel also has 3 million telephone lines.[10] More than 4.5 million Israelis enjoy surfing the

Visitors to the Dead Sea smear themselves in the mineral-rich mud to take advantage of its benefits.

Internet.[11] Television programs in the country are broadcast in both Hebrew and Arabic.[12] There is also a Russian language channel for Israel's many Russian immigrants, a music channel, and a channel that allows Israelis to monitor the goings-on in the Knesset.

The country's transportation system is well developed, with a network of roads and highways linking Israel's cities. Public transportation consists of buses, taxis, and minibuses called *sheruts* that are like shared taxis. Israel boasts 605 miles (975 km) of railroads.[13] Air traffic comes and goes regularly into and out of Israel's 48 airports. The country's main airport, stationed outside Tel Aviv, is Ben-Gurion International Airport. Most of Israel's goods are shipped by air or water. Haifa, Elat, and Ashdod are the country's major ports. They provide access to trade routes to Europe, Asia, and Africa. Hundreds of miles of pipelines allow Israel to transport natural gas, oil, water, and other resources across the country.

ECONOMIC INEQUALITY

Despite Israel's overall wealth, more than 20 percent of Israelis live in poverty.[14] This is partly due to the fact that many families—particularly among Arabs and ultraorthodox Jews—struggle to support many children on one income. Arab women are often discouraged from entering the workforce, and many Haredi men choose to study religion rather than work. Both of these groups tend to have larger-than-average families. In addition, many immigrants have trouble finding employment, and discrimination against Arabs and Oriental Jews means they tend to be offered the least desirable and lowest paid jobs. Recent cuts in welfare benefits have also contributed to an increase in poverty.

CHAPTER 9
ISRAEL TODAY

The people who call Israel their home today are divided by ethnicity, religion, and politics. They are also united by the history, experiences, and challenges they share. As Israel moves further into the twenty-first century, its social barriers are gradually breaking down, and a distinct Israeli culture is emerging.

The majority of Israelis today did not arrive from far-off places. They were born and raised in the country, and more and more come from mixed backgrounds. These native-born Israelis, or Sabras, grew up in a country surrounded by hostility, and they fought side by side to protect their homeland. These experiences have brought them closer together. Sabras have developed a reputation for appearing tough on the outside. Yet, like the prickly pear for which they are named, they are soft inside, valuing family, community, and tradition.

Israelis can legally enter the workforce at age 15.

This image depicts the Israel-Palestine struggle, showing the flags of the two states overlapping.

BAR AND BAT MITZVAHS

As they near or enter their teenage years, most Jews participate in a religious ceremony that marks their transition into adulthood. For Jewish boys, the ceremony is called a bar mitzvah. Traditionally, after a period of preparation, a Jewish boy will be called on to read from the Torah on the first Sabbath after his thirteenth birthday. This ritual demonstrates the fact that he is now old enough to take on full responsibility for following Jewish law. The boy's family gathers to listen to the reading, and there is often a celebration afterward. Many Jewish girls participate in a similar ceremony called a bat mitzvah when they turn 12. In Israel, the Western Wall is a popular place for bar and bat mitzvah festivities.

The average Israeli family tends to be larger than in other developed nations due to religious and cultural beliefs. Communities are close-knit. People are informal with one another and can be brutally honest. And even to the most progressive and least religious Israelis, tradition is a cherished part of life.

Modern Israel is a cosmopolitan nation. International influences are welcomed and quickly woven into the fabric of Israeli culture. Western culture is the most prominent and can be seen in everything from clothing to the political process. Capitalism, materialism, and secularism are gaining ground. At the same time, Israel retains a passionate—and sometimes aggressive—devotion to its land and religious

A Jewish boy celebrates his bar mitzvah at the Western Wall.

traditions. Israelis take great pride in their country and feel a special solidarity with their fellow citizens.

ISRAELI TEENS

Teens in Israel love to have fun. However, Israeli teens also feel a sense of duty to their families, communities, and country. Most teens live in bustling cities, often in apartment buildings. Before they learn to drive at 17, they can get around using public transportation. Teens are aware of the possibility of terrorist attacks, but they generally do not let that stop them from visiting friends and hanging out in crowded public places such as restaurants, movie theaters, and malls. At home, if their chores and homework are done, many teens rely on high-tech

DATING

Israeli teens are usually allowed to go on dates, although dating is more complicated for Orthodox Jewish and Muslim teens. In their late teens or early twenties, Orthodox Jews start looking for a spouse. A family member, friend, or professional matchmaker sets them up with a date—usually a stranger. They must follow strict rules while dating, including never touching and never being alone together. The couple has between a few days and several months to decide whether they will get engaged.

Muslim teens are also forbidden to spend time alone with dates. In conservative Muslim communities, teens may not be allowed to date at all. Instead, marriages are arranged by teens' families.

entertainment. They go online, call or text their friends, watch television, or listen to music.

Teens who live in rural communities, such as kibbutzim and moshavim, contribute by working on the farm. Those from large or poverty-stricken families may take jobs early to contribute to the household income. A majority of Israeli teens also contribute to their country's security by serving in the military.

EDUCATION AND THE MILITARY

Israelis are required to attend school between the ages of five and 15, and approximately 85 percent go on to complete secondary school.[1] Parents can enroll their children in secular or religious schools. Even secular schools teach the basics of Jewish culture and history, while religious schools provide a more in-depth religious curriculum and practice stricter adherence to Jewish law. In Jewish schools, classes are taught in Hebrew. Separate schools for Israeli Arabs focus on Arab culture, history, and Islam. Teachers in Arab schools use Arabic.

After graduating from high school at approximately age 18, nearly all Jewish, Druze, and Circassian Israelis—including women—must serve in the Israel Defense Forces (IDF). Some Orthodox Jewish men and women are allowed to pursue religious studies or community service instead. Israeli Arabs are not required to serve in the IDF, although

More than 97 percent of Israelis over the age of 15 can read and write.[2]

some volunteer to do so. Men must devote at least 28 months to military service, and women must serve for at least 18 months. Most Israelis are proud and willing to serve their country. Afterward, it is a tradition for Israelis to travel the world before going to college or joining the workforce. Forty-two percent of Israelis further their education after serving in the military.[3]

CURRENT ISSUES

In 2012, Israel remained swept up in the political unrest in the Middle East. The peace process between Israelis and Palestinians had stalled, making the likelihood of Israel's right-wing government renewing negotiations with the PA slim. Prime Minister Netanyahu's support

Young women in Israel's army take a break during training.

of Jewish settlements in the West Bank had angered Palestinians and perhaps diminished the chance for a peaceful and permanent resolution to the Israeli-Palestinian conflict.

Tensions between Israel and other Arab nations had also intensified. A violent civil war in neighboring Syria had threatened to spill over the Israeli border. Relations with Egypt had cooled after the country terminated its agreement to supply Israel with natural gas. In addition, the widespread fear that Iran had begun manufacturing nuclear weapons—which the Islamic country might use to destroy the Jewish State of Israel—had Israel on edge and ready to strike out in defense despite pressure from other nations to keep the peace.

Within Israel, ethnic conflicts had focused on immigration. Tens of thousands of African immigrants had entered Israel illegally over the past several years. Some had come in hopes of finding better employment, while others sought political asylum. The influx of immigrants had touched off a debate between Israelis who believed these newcomers threaten society and those who believed in offering them refuge. As of June 2012, Israel was set to begin deporting some of the illegal immigrants.

A recent increase in violent crime had also plagued the country. Some Israelis blamed the problem on foreigners.

In June 2012, an African man protested Israel's policy regarding African immigrants.

ISRAEL'S FUTURE

Israel's future is uncertain, yet hopeful. The Israeli-Palestinian conflict and wider Arab-Israeli conflict have gone on for so long, and with such rigidity on both sides, that many Israelis have given up hope for peace. And though the gaps between Israel's ethnic groups are slowly narrowing, Israelis will need to work hard to eradicate long-standing prejudices.

Despite these ongoing struggles, Israel has proven to be a strong, successful, and resilient nation of hard workers and innovative thinkers. Each new generation of Israelis brings with it a chance to move toward a culture of integration, inclusion, and mutual respect—a chance for a peaceful future. After all, whether they are Jewish or Arab, Israelis are more alike than they are different. They all simply want a place to call home.

LEARNING TOGETHER

Today, several schools in Israel are working to integrate Jewish and Arab students. An organization called Hand in Hand was founded in 1997 and has since opened three bilingual schools in which Jewish and Arab students learn together. Hebrew schools are also making an effort to teach students about the Arab culture and language by hiring Arab teachers and welcoming Arab students.

The Israeli-Palestinian conflict affects everyone—young and old—in Israel.

TIMELINE

8000 BCE	Humans build cities, including Jericho, in Palestine.
2000 BCE	Abraham settles in Canaan, the area later known as Palestine, around this time.
1250 BCE	Moses leads the Israelites out of Egypt and back to their promised land.
965 BCE	Solomon builds the first Jewish temple in Jerusalem.
63 BCE	The Romans seize Jerusalem.
66 CE	The Romans crush the Jews' rebellion, leaving only the Western Wall of the Second Temple, and cast out surviving Jews from Jerusalem.
638	Arabs conquer Jerusalem.
1516	Ottoman Turks conquer Palestine.
1880s	The Zionist movement begins.
1918	World War I ends and Palestine is created by the British, who want Jews and Arabs to share the country.
1945	World War II ends, leaving many Holocaust survivors seeking refuge in Palestine.
1948	Israel declares its independence as a Jewish state on May 14.

1949	Israel wins the War of Independence, and hundreds of thousands of Arabs flee the country.
1958	The Knesset passes the first of Israel's Basic Laws.
1967	Israel seizes territory from Egypt, Jordan, and Syria in the Six-Day War, fought June 5–10.
1973	The Yom Kippur War plunges Israel into an economic recession and isolates it from many of its allies.
1982	Israel wins a war against PLO forces in Lebanon.
1987–1988	In an event called the intifada, Palestinians riot against Jews in the West Bank and the Gaza Strip.
1988	PLO leader Yasser Arafat recognizes Israel's right to exist and promises to stop terrorist activity.
1993–1994	The Oslo Accords lay the foundation for peace between Israelis and Palestinians, including granting autonomy to Palestinians.
2000	A second intifada breaks out, highlighting tensions between Israelis and Palestinians.
2002	The Israeli government approves construction of a security fence between Israel and the West Bank.
2007	The Islamic group Hamas takes over the Gaza Strip and begins attacking Israel; violence continues for a couple years.
2011	Uprisings across the Middle East and protests in Israel result in political turmoil.

FACTS AT YOUR FINGERTIPS

GEOGRAPHY

Official name: State of Israel
(in Hebrew, Medinat Ysra'el;
in Arabic, Isra'il)

Area: 8,019 square miles
(20,770 sq km)

Climate: hot, dry desert in the
south and east; cooler along the
Mediterranean coast and in the
north

Highest elevation: Mount Meron,
3,963 feet (1,208 m) above sea level

Lowest elevation: the Dead Sea,
1,339 feet (408 m) below sea level

Significant geographic features:
Dead Sea, Great Rift Valley, Negev
Desert

PEOPLE

Population (July 2012 est.):
7,590,758

Most populous city: Tel Aviv

Ethnic groups: Jewish, 76.4 percent;
non-Jewish (mostly Arab), 23.6
percent

Percentage of residents living in
urban areas: 92 percent

Life expectancy: 81.07 years at birth
(world rank: 18)

Languages: Hebrew (official), Arabic
(official for Arab minority), English

Religions: Jewish, 75.6 percent;
Muslim, 16.9 percent; Christian, 2
percent; Druze, 1.7 percent; other,
3.8 percent

GOVERNMENT AND ECONOMY

Government: parliamentary democracy

Capital: Jerusalem

Date of adoption of current constitution: no written constitution

Head of state: president

Head of government: prime minister

Legislature: Knesset

Currency: new Israeli shekel

Industries and natural resources: chemicals, finished diamonds, high-tech products, pharmaceuticals, copper ore, natural gas, phosphates, potash

NATIONAL SYMBOLS

Holidays: Rosh Hashanah (September or October), Yom Kippur (September or October), Independence Day (April or May)

Flag: A white background with blue horizontal bands near the top and bottom and a blue six-pointed star in the center. The star is the Shield of David. Israel's flag design is similar to that of the traditional Jewish prayer shawl.

National anthem: "Hatikvah" ("The Hope")

National bird: hoopoe

KEY PEOPLE

Abraham (early second millennium BCE), founder of the Jewish people

Theodor Herzl (1860–1904), founder of political Zionism

David Ben-Gurion (1886–1973), Israel's first prime minister, serving from 1948 to 1953 and again from 1955 to 1963

Yasser Arafat (1929–2004), leader of the PLO and first president of the PA, initiated the peace process with the Israeli government

Benjamin Netanyahu (1949–present), prime minister and leader of the Likud Party; also served as prime minister from 1996 to 1999

DISTRICTS OF ISRAEL

District; Capital

Central; Ramla

Haifa; Haifa

Jerusalem; Jerusalem

Northern; Nazareth

Southern; Beersheba

Tel Aviv; Tel Aviv

GLOSSARY

anti-Semitism
> Hostility toward Jews.

asylum
> Protection offered by one government against another.

centrist
> Of the center or moderate in politics.

coalition
> A temporary alliance of political parties or other groups that agree to work toward a common goal.

collective
> Shared equally among all members of a group.

gross domestic product
> A measure of a country's economy; the total of all goods and services produced in a country in a year.

infrastructure
> A nation's system of public services and resources, such as roads and buses.

left wing
> The more liberal—less traditional—division of a group, especially of a political party.

menorah
> A candleholder with either seven or nine candles used in Jewish religious rituals.

monotheistic
> Believing in only one God.

mystical
> Spiritual; involving communion with God.

nationalist
> Of or having to do with the interests of one's nation.

orthodox
> Adhering to tradition or religious law.

potash
> A form of potassium often used as fertilizer and to make soap.

reparation
> Financial compensation for damages sustained in war.

right wing
> The more conservative division of a group, especially of a political party.

tribunal
> A court in a specific area, such as a religion or the military.

ADDITIONAL RESOURCES

SELECTED BIBLIOGRAPHY

Fodor's Israel. New York: Fodor's Travel, 2011. Print.

"The World Factbook: Israel." *Central Intelligence Agency.* Central Intelligence Agency, 13 Apr. 2012. Web. 9 May 2012.

"Israel." *Encyclopædia Britannica.* Encyclopædia Britannica, 2012. Web. 9 May 2012.

Reich, Bernard. *A Brief History of Israel.* 2nd ed. New York: Checkmark, 2008. Print.

Rubin, Barry M. *Israel: An Introduction.* New Haven, CT: Yale UP, 2012. Print.

FURTHER READINGS

Ellis, Deborah. *Three Wishes: Palestinian and Israeli Children Speak.* Toronto, ON: Groundwood, 2004. Print.

Harms, Gregory, and Todd M. Ferry. *The Palestine-Israel Conflict: A Basic Introduction.* 3rd ed. Ann Arbor, MI: Pluto, 2012. Print.

Wiesel, Elie. *Night.* trans. Marion Wiesel. New York: Hill and Wang, 2006. Print.

WEB LINKS

To learn more about Israel, visit ABDO Publishing Company online at **www.abdopublishing.com**. Web sites about Israel are featured on our Book Links page. These links are routinely monitored and updated to provide the most current information available.

PLACES TO VISIT

If you are ever in Israel, consider checking out these important and interesting sites!

Dead Sea

This body of water in eastern Israel is renowned for its healing minerals. Tourists enjoy floating in the sea and coating themselves in soothing mud.

Israel Museum

The largest museum in Israel, located in Jerusalem, has separate wings devoted to archaeology, fine arts, and Jewish culture. The Dead Sea Scrolls are also housed there.

Temple Mount

This complex in Jerusalem's Old City encompasses some of the holiest sites in Judaism and Islam, including the Western Wall and the Dome of the Rock.

Yad Vashem

This museum and memorial to victims of the Holocaust includes a history museum, an art museum, an education center, and a synagogue.

SOURCE NOTES

CHAPTER 1. A VISIT TO ISRAEL

1. "The World Factbook: Israel." *Central Intelligence Agency*. Central Intelligence Agency, 13 Apr. 2012. Web. 9 May 2012.

CHAPTER 2. GEOGRAPHY: A VARIED LANDSCAPE

1. "The World Factbook: Israel." *Central Intelligence Agency*. Central Intelligence Agency, 13 Apr. 2012. Web. 9 May 2012.

2. "Israel." *Encyclopædia Britannica*. Encyclopædia Britannica, 2012. Web. 9 May 2012.

3. Barry M. Rubin. *Israel: An Introduction*. New Haven, CT: Yale UP, 2012. Print. 109.

4. Ibid.

5. "Israel." *Encyclopædia Britannica*. Encyclopædia Britannica, 2012. Web. 9 May 2012.

6. "Haifa, Israel." *Weatherbase*. Canty and Associates, 2012. Web. 12 Aug. 2012.

7. "Jerusalem, Israel." *Weatherbase*. Canty and Associates, 2012. Web. 12 Aug. 2012.

8. "Beersheva, Israel." *Weatherbase*. Canty and Associates, 2012. Web. 12 Aug. 2012.

9. "Eilat, Israel." *Weatherbase*. Canty and Associates, 2012. Web. 12 Aug. 2012.

CHAPTER 3. ANIMALS AND NATURE: PARADISE REGAINED

1. "*Gazella gazella*." *IUCN Red List*. IUCN, 2011. Web. 22 May 2012.

2. Kari Lee. "*Gazella gazelle*." *Animal Diversity Web*. Regents of the University of Michigan, 2012. Web. 22 May 2012.

3. "Israel." *Encyclopædia Britannica*. Encyclopædia Britannica, 2012. Web. 23 May 2012.

4. Barry M. Rubin. *Israel: An Introduction*. New Haven, CT: Yale UP, 2012. Print. 102.

5. "Hula Valley." *Encyclopædia Britannica*. Encyclopædia Britannica, 2012. Web. 24 May 2012.

6. Jon Donnison. "Bird Watchers Find Heaven in 'Superhighway' Israel." *BBC*. BBC, 1 Dec. 2012. Web. 23 May 2012.

7. "Hoopoe." *Encyclopædia Britannica*. Encyclopædia Britannica, 2012. Web. 24 May 2012.

8. Barry M. Rubin. *Israel: An Introduction*. New Haven, CT: Yale UP, 2012. Print. 102.

9. Ibid.

10. "Forestry and Ecology." *Jewish National Fund*. Jewish National Fund, n.d. Web. 23 May 2012.

11. "Water Projects." *Jewish National Fund.* Jewish National Fund, n.d. Web. 23 May 2012.

12. "Summary Statistics: Summaries by Country, Table 5: Threatened Species in Each Country." *IUCN Red List of Threatened Species.* International Union for Conservation of Nature and Natural Resources, 2011. Web. 18 Sept. 2012.

CHAPTER 4. HISTORY: THE BATTLE FOR THE HOLY LAND

1. Bernard Reich. *A Brief History of Israel.* 2nd ed. New York: Checkmark, 2008. Print. 13–17.

2. Ibid. 34–35.

3. "Intifada." *M-W.com.* Merriam-Webster, 2012. Web. 18 Sept. 2012.

4. Barry M. Rubin. *Israel: An Introduction.* New Haven, CT: Yale UP, 2012. Print. 63–35.

CHAPTER 5. PEOPLE: A NATION OF IMMIGRANTS

1. Barry M. Rubin. *Israel: An Introduction.* New Haven, CT: Yale UP, 2012. Print. 106.

2. "The World Factbook: Israel." *Central Intelligence Agency.* Central Intelligence Agency, 13 Apr. 2012. Web. 9 May 2012.

3. Ibid.

4. "Israel." *Encyclopædia Britannica.* Encyclopædia Britannica, 2012. Web. 12 Aug. 2012

5. Ibid.

6. "The World Factbook: Israel." *Central Intelligence Agency.* Central Intelligence Agency, 4 Oct. 2012. Web. 17 Oct. 2012.

7. "Israel." *Encyclopædia Britannica.* Encyclopædia Britannica, 2012. Web. 28 May 2012.

8. Peter W. Williams. "Christianity." *World Book Advanced.* World Book, 2012. Web. 25 May 2012.

9. "The World Factbook: Israel." *Central Intelligence Agency.* Central Intelligence Agency, 13 Apr. 2012. Web. 9 May 2012.

10. "Jerusalem." *Encyclopædia Britannica.* Encyclopædia Britannica, 2012. Web. 26 May 2012.

11. Isabel Kershner. "Crackdown on Migrants Tugs at Soul of Israelis." *New York Times.* New York Times, 18 June 2012. Web. 10 July 2012.

12. "Falasha." *Encyclopædia Britannica.* Encyclopædia Britannica, 2012. Web. 10 July 2012.

SOURCE NOTES CONTINUED

CHAPTER 6. CULTURE: SHAPED BY DIFFERENCES

None.

CHAPTER 7. POLITICS: A JEWISH DEMOCRACY

1. "The World Factbook: Israel." *Central Intelligence Agency*. Central Intelligence Agency, 13 Apr. 2012. Web. 9 May 2012.

2. Ibid.

3. Ibid.

4. "Palestinian Election." *Encyclopædia Britannica*. Encyclopædia Britannica, 2012. Web. 7 June 2012.

5. Bernard Reich. *A Brief History of Israel*. 2nd ed. New York: Checkmark, 2008. Print. 47.

CHAPTER 8. ECONOMICS: A SELF-MADE NATION

1. "The World Factbook: Israel." *Central Intelligence Agency*. Central Intelligence Agency, 13 Apr. 2012. Web. 9 May 2012.

2. Barry M. Rubin. *Israel: An Introduction*. New Haven, CT: Yale UP, 2012. Print. 251.

3. "The World Factbook: Israel." *Central Intelligence Agency*. Central Intelligence Agency, 13 Apr. 2012. Web. 9 May 2012.

4. Ibid.

5. "Israel." *Encyclopædia Britannica*. Encyclopædia Britannica, 2012. Web. 7 June 2012.

6. "The World Factbook: Israel." *Central Intelligence Agency*. Central Intelligence Agency, 13 Apr. 2012. Web. 9 May 2012.

7. Marcy Oster. "Tourists Flocking to Israel at Record Pace." *JTA*. JTA, 20 July 2010. Web. 10 June 2012.

8. "Israel." *Encyclopædia Britannica*. Encyclopædia Britannica, 2012. Web. 10 June 2012.

9. Ibid.

10. "The World Factbook: Israel." *Central Intelligence Agency*. Central Intelligence Agency, 13 Apr. 2012. Web. 9 May 2012.

11. Ibid.

12. Ibid.

13. Ibid.

14. Ibid.

CHAPTER 9. ISRAEL TODAY

1. Barry M. Rubin. *Israel: An Introduction*. New Haven, CT: Yale UP, 2012. Print. 179.

2. "The World Factbook: Israel." *Central Intelligence Agency*. Central Intelligence Agency, 13 Apr. 2012. Web. 9 May 2012.

3. Barry M. Rubin. *Israel: An Introduction*. New Haven, CT: Yale UP, 2012. Print. 178–180.

4. "At a Glance: Israel." *UNICEF*. UNICEF, 2010. Web. 12 June 2012.

5. Ibid.

6. "Country Statistical Profile: Israel." *OECD*. OECD, 2011. Web. 12 June 2012.

INDEX

INDEX CONTINUED

PHOTO CREDITS